Concepts In C

Chandra Prakash

Dedicated to my beloved parents

Arun Kumar Singh

Indu Devi

&

My inspiration and ideal

Narasimha Karumanchi

Sandeep Jain

Acknowledgments

I would like to express my sincere gratitude to many people who were with me during writing this book. Also to all those people who helped me directly or indirectly like in editing, proofreading, cover page designing and book's content design. In particular, my sincere thanks go to following people.

Narasimha Karumanchi [M.Tech IIT Mumbai, Founder at CarrerMonk.com] my inspiration and ideal who not only helped when I was in need but also encouraged and supported me a lot every time. I can never forget his help and support. I really want to thank him from the depth of my heart.

Sandeep Jain [Owner at geeksforgeeks.org] for his encouragement and support during those days when I used to write articles on Data Structure & Algorithm for geeksforgeeks. He has also motivated me a lot. I would also like to thank and congratulate him again for geeksforgeeks.org and geeksquiz.com. These two sites helped me a lot while I was writing my book.

My college friends- Jitesh Kumar [Tata Consultancy Services], Nishant Saurbh, Sujeet Kumar, Vivekanand Jha and all other friends who have contributed to the quality of this book. Many thanks for your support, help and suggestion.

-Chandra Prakash

Contents

Introduction

The book "Concepts In C" is not like those textbooks available in the market toady where only problems are given with their answers but explanations are missing. This book will actually let you know about every aspect of C. Around 400+ questions are given with their answers as well as brief explanation. All questions are of good standard and cover almost every important and hot topics of C language.

Before going through this book, I must say if you don't have basic knowledge of C then don't read this. First of all, be clear with the basics of C. This book will become a boon for those who have desire to be a proficient programmer in C language. Topics like Pointer, Array, String, Structure, Union, Enum contains a lot of problems which will hone your skill in C language.

Topics like Complicated Declaration, Variadic Function, Variable Number Of Arguments, Memory Management and Miscellaneous Concepts will take you to the next level of C language. You rarely find these topics in other books but Concepts In C have taken care of such interesting and hot topics of C.

This book is a bible for those who are preparing for Campus interviews and preparing for other competitive examinations.

If anyone finds any error or typo in the book, kindly let me know. Also if you have any query, problem or suggestion, please feel free to contact me at- cpbcrec@gmail.com.

CHANDRA PRAKASH

Chapter-1

Variables, Declarations & Initializations

Q1.What will be the output of below C program?

```
#include <stdio.h>

int main()

{

int a;

int x = 4;

printf ("%d %d\n", a, x);

return 0;

}
```

Answer: GARBAGE VALUE, 4

First statement **int a** is a declaration where **a** has been declared as a variable of type **integer(int)** and has not been initialized with any value so it contains garbage value whereas in second line, **x** has been declared as well as initialized with a value 4 in this case so variable **x** contains 4.

Q2.What will be the output of below C code?

```
#include <stdio.h>

int main()

{

int a = 4;

a = 6;

a = 8;
```

printf ("Final value of a is: %d\n", a);

return 0;

}

Answer: Final value of a is: 8

Here variable **a** has been initially initialized with 4 but in next two consecutive lines this value has been changed to 6 and 8. Since final value is 8 that has been given to **a**. So, **printf** () prints 8.

Q3. What will be the output of below C code in Turbo C++?

#include <stdio.h>

int main()

{

int a = b = c = d = 10;

printf ("%d %d %d %d\n", a, b, c, d);

return 0;

}

Answer: Compilation error.

Here we are trying to use **b** (to assign to **a**) before defining it. Rule says that we cannot use any variable before defining it properly.

We can modify the above code as to work properly as-

int a, b, c, d;

a = b = c = d = 10;

Q4. What would be the output of below C program?

#include <stdio.h>

```
int main()

{

int a = 1 , 2;

printf ("%d\n", a);

return 0;

}
```

Answer:

Compilation error:-"Declaration terminated incorrectly in function **main** ()".

Assignment operator has higher precedence than comma. Comma acts as a separator here. The compiler creates an integer variable and initializes it with 1. The compiler fails to create integer variable 2 because 2 is not a valid identifier.

Q5.What would be the output of below C code?

```
#include <stdio.h>

int main()

{

int a = (1 , 2);

printf ("%d\n", a);

return 0;

}
```

Answer: 2

Here parenthesis, solve our problem and also comma operator works. Due this, the value which has been assigned to variable **a** is 2.

Don't need to worry about comma operator and all. We will explore more about these all in coming chapters. Things will get clear soon.

Q6. What do you understand by scope of a variable? Also mention different types of scopes of a variable in C.

Answer:

A scope is the context within a computer program in which a variable name or other identifier is valid and can be used, or within which a declaration has effect. Outside of the scope of a variable name, the variable's value may still be stored, and may even be accessible in some way, but the name does not refer to it; that is, the name is not bound to the variable's storage.

There are four kinds of scopes mainly in C and they are:

File, Function, Block and Prototype.

Q7. What will be the output of below C code?

```c
#include <stdio.h>

int x=4;

int main()
{
int x=6;
printf ("%d\n", x);
return 0;
}
```

Answer: 6

Here we have two scopes related with variable **x**. One is **global** and other one is **local**. Whenever there is a conflict between a variable having local scope and global scope then the **local** variable gets a priority.

Q8. What would be the output of the following program?

```c
#include <stdio.h>

int main()

{

int x=10;

{

int x = 20;

printf ("%d\n", x);

}

printf ("%d\n", x);

return 0;

}
```

Answer: 20

       10

Here there is a conflict between two local variables. But the one that is more local gets the priority. More local means the one that is nearer to the point of usage. Here point of usage is the call of **printf** () function.

Q9. What will be the output of below C code?

```c
#include <stdio.h>

int main()

{
```

int a=10;

printf ("%d", printf ("%d %d %d", a, a, a));

return 0;

}

Answer: 10 10 10 5

The concept hidden in this program is return type of **printf** () function. The **printf** () always return the number of character printed. Here inner **printf** () is first called which print value of **a** three times with space between each value, 10, 10, 10. Total numbers of five characters get printed (3 value of 10 and 2 spaces). And this returned value i, e 5 is finally printed by outer **printf** ().

Q10. What is the return type of printf () and scanf () in C?

1) void

2) int

3) float

4) char

The return type of **printf** () and **scanf** () is int.

In the following declaration, observe the return type is **int**.

int printf(const char *format, ...);
int scanf(const char *format, ...);

printf () returns the number of characters printed on the console
scanf () returns the number of variables to which you are providing the input.

Q11. What will be the output of below C code?

```c
#include <stdio.h>

int main()

{

int i = 43;

printf ("%d\n", printf("%d", printf("%d", i)));

return 0;

}
```

Answer: 4321

Explanation is same as above.

Q12. What will be the output of following C code?

```c
#include <stdio.h>

int main()

{

float f = 43.98;

int k;

k = printf ("%f ", f);

printf ("\n%d", k);

return 0;

}
```

Answer: 43.980000 9

First **printf** () prints a float value corresponding to variable **f** and returns 9 (number of characters printed on console) which is being printed by second **printf** ().

Q13. What will be the output of below C code?

```
#include <stdio.h>
int main()

{
int a = 0, b = 0;

a = (b = 75) + 9;

printf ("\n%d %d", a, b);

return 0;

}
```

Answer: 84 75

Q14. What will be the output of below C program?

```
#include <stdio.h>

int main()

{
int i;

for (; scanf ("%d", &i); printf ("%d", i));

return 0;

}
```

Answer: This program goes into infinite loop. Because **scanf** () in **for** loop would act as result of condition. And since return type of **scanf** () is always

int so test condition will always be true and hence program goes in infinite loop.

Q15. Which of the following is integral data type?

    1) void

    2) char

    3) double

    4) float

Answer: char

In C whenever we assign a value in **char** type variable then ASCII value corresponding to that variable gets stored and ASCII value is of integral type. So **char** is of integral data type.

Q16. What will be the output of below C program?

#include <stdio.h>

int main()

{

 int i;

int a = 10;

printf ("%d %d", a, scanf ("%d", &i));

return 0;

}

Answer: 10   1

Concept used here is that C's calling convention is from right to left. So first **scanf** () gets executed it receives something but return an integral value i, e 1 in this case. Once **printf** () collects them, it prints them in the order in which we have asked.

Q17. What is the difference between a declaration and a definition of a variable?

a) Both can occur multiple times, but a declaration must occur first.

b) There is no difference between them.

c) A definition occurs once, but a declaration may occur many times.

d) A declaration occurs once, but a definition may occur many times.

Answer: (c)

Explanation-

In the definition of a variable space is reserved and some initial value is given to that variable whereas declaration only identifies the type of variable. Its definition that tells about where the variable is created or assigned storage, declaration merely refers to place where nature of variable is stated.

Note: - **redefinition is an error but re-declaration is not an error**.

Q18. Which of the following statement is a declaration and which is a definition?

extern int i;

int j;

Answer:

First one is a declaration

Second one is a definition.

Q19. Identify the correct output for the program given below.

#include <stdio.h>

int main()

{

extern int i;

i = 10;

i = 20;

printf ("%d\n", i);

return 0;

}

a) 20

b) 10

c) Error i undefined

d) None of these

Answer: c

As stated above, **extern int** is a declaration not a definition hence, an error.

Q20. Is it true that a global variable and a function may have several declarations but only one definition? [Yes/No]

Answer: Yes.

As explained above redefinition in an error not re declaration.

Q21. What will be the output of below C program?

#include <stdio.h>

int main()

{

extern int i;

printf ("%d", i);

return 0;

}

int i = 10;

Answer: 10

As **extern int i** is a declaration, whereas int i = 10 is the definition.

Q22. What is the difference between the following C statements?

extern int fun();

int fun();

Answers:

Both statements are declarations and there is no difference except for the fact that the first one gives a hint that the function func() is present in other source file.

extern mainly implies the storage class of a variable. We will explore more on storage class in C and their uses in coming questions.

Q23. What are the different data types in C.? Also mention the memory space they occupy on different systems. (16-bit/32-bit)

Answer:

- signed char -   1 byte.
- unsigned char –   1 byte.
- short signed int - 2 byte.
- short unsigned int- 2 byte.
- signed int-   2 byte.
- unsigned int-   2 byte.
- long unsigned int- 4 byte.

- long signed int-   4 byte.
- float-   4 byte.
- double-   8 byte.
- long double-   10 byte.

Note: - The sizes of **short, int, long** are compiler dependent. Sizes given above are for 16-bit compiler.

Q24. What is the memory size taken by short int and long int.?

Answer: **short int** always take 2 bytes irrespective of system whereas **long int** always occupy 4 bytes regardless of system architecture.

Q25. Will the below C program compile successfully?

#include <stdio.h>

int main()

{

char *ptr1 , c;

void *ptr2 , v;

c = 10, v = 20;

ptr1 = &c;

ptr2 = &v;

return 0;

}

Answer: No. The program will not compile. The concept is that in C, we may have a **void** pointer (we will explore more on pointers and their types in pointer chapter) but we can't declare a **void** data type. Compiler issues an error because compiler does not know how much memory space should be allocated for such types of variable.

Q26. What do you mean by storage class of a variable? What are the different types of data storage class in C?

Answer: From C compiler's point of view, a variable name identifies some physical location within the computer where the strings of bits representing the variable's value are stored. So it's the storage class which decides where to store the variable. Basically there are two kinds of locations in a computer where variables are stored- Memory and CPU registers.

Moreover, a variable's storage class tells us:

1. Where the variable would be stored.

2. What will be the initial value of the variable, if initial value is no specifically assigned (i, e the default initial value).

3. What is the scope of the variable i, e in which function the value of variable would be available.

4. What is the life of the variable i, e how long would the variable exist.

There are four storage classes in C:

a) Automatic storage class.

b) Register storage class.

c) Static storage class.

d) External storage class (extern).

Let us examine these storage classes one by one.

Automatic Storage class

Storage	Memory (RAM)
Default initial value	Garbage value
Scope	Local to the block in which the variable is defined.
Life	Till the control remains within the block in which the variable is defined.

14

Register Storage class

Storage	CPU registers
Default initial value	Garbage value
Scope	Local to the block in which the variable is defined.
Life	Till the control remains within the block in which the variable is defined.

Static Storage Class

Storage	Memory (Data Segment)
Default initial value	Zero
Scope	Local to the block in which the variable is defined.
Life	Value of the variable persists between different function calls.

External storage Class

Storage	Memory
Default initial value	Zero
Scope	Global
Life	As long as the program's execution doesn't come to an end.

Q27. What is the storage class of **i** in the following statement?

    int i;

Answer: The storage class of variable **i** is **auto** if it is declared within **main** () and extern if declared outside **main** ().

Note: - Default values stored in any variables depend upon where they are defined. Default storage class any variable is **auto** unless explicitly qualified.

Q28. What will be the output of following C program?

```c
#include <stdio.h>
int i;
int main()
{
int k;
printf ("Let's see how storage class works!\n");
{
int i = 10;
k = printf ("Value of i is: %d\n", i);
}
printf ("Sum of global i and local k is : %d", i + k);
return 0;
}
```

Answer: Let's see how storage class works!

       Value of i is: 10

       Sum of global i and local k is: 19

Here variable **i** has been defined in two different scopes. These two **i** are completely different. According to storage class concept **i** is defined above **main** (), has default initial value equal to zero but **i** defined inside **main** () has 10 in it. Rest of the program is straight forward.

Note:-Also think about return type of **printf** () in this program.

Q29. What is sizeof () in C?

Answer: C provides a compile-time unary operator called **sizeof** that can be used to compute the size of any object. The expressions-

sizeof (object) and

sizeof (type name) yield an integer equal to the size of the specified object or type in bytes. (Strictly, sizeof produces an unsigned integer value whose type, size_t, is defined in the header <stddef.h>) An object can be a variable or array or structure. A type name can be the name of a basic type like **int** or **double**, or a derived type like a **structure** or a **pointer**.

Q30. What is size_t in C?

Answer: Unsigned integral type and alias of one of the fundamental unsigned integer types. It is a type able to represent the size of any object in bytes: **size_t** is the type returned by the sizeof operator and is widely used in the standard library to represent sizes and counts.

For example, it is the type that you pass to **malloc** () to indicate how many bytes you want to allocate.

Q31. What will be the output of below C program?

#include <stdio.h>

int main()

{

printf ("%d\t", sizeof(6.5));

printf ("%d\t", sizeof(6.5f));

printf ("%d\t", sizeof(1000));

printf ("%d", sizeof('A'));

return 0;

}

Answer: 8 4 2 2

By default data type of numeric constants is double. Hence **sizeof** (6.5) returns memory occupied by a double and hence first **printf** () prints 8. In second **printf** (), **sizeof** () returns size of a **float** type, hence output is 4. Third one is an integer, hence output is obvious. In last statement we have a character constant. A character constant always occupy 2 bytes of memory and hence the output.

Note: - In C a character constant is of **int** type and what actually gets stored in memory is ASCII value of that character constant.

Q32. Will the program given below compile successfully?

#include <stdio.h>

int main()

{

printf ("%d", sizeof ('ABC'));

return 0;

}

Answer: No, there will be a compilation error- "character constant must be one or two characters long in function **main** ()".

So inside **sizeof** () character operand should be one or two character long otherwise an error will be thrown.

Note: - Think what will happen if we replace 'ABC' by "ABC" inside **sizeof** () operator.

Q33. What will be the output of the following C program?

```c
#include<stdio.h>
int main()
{
struct xx
{
int x = 3;
char name[] = "Hello";
};
struct xx *s;
printf ("%d", s->x);
printf ("%s", s->name);

return 0;
}
```

Answer: Compile Time Error.

Concept is that we can't initialize variables in declaration. Structure declaration is just like a template, it doesn't tell the compiler to reserve any space inside memory. All a structure declaration does is, it defines the 'form' of the structure.

Q34. What will be the output of below C code?

```c
#include <stdio.h>

int i;

int main()

{
int t;
for (t = 4; scanf ("%d", &i) - t ; printf ("%d\n", i))
printf("%d--", t--);
```

```
return 0;
}
```

Answer: If the inputs are 0,1,2,3 then answer will be-

4--0

3--1

2--2

Explanation: -

Let us assume for some x = scanf ("%d", &i) - t then, values during execution

will be-

t	i	x
4	0	-4
3	1	-2
2	2	0

Q35. What will be the output of below C program?

```
#include <stdio.h>

int main()

{

struct emp

{

char name[20];

int age;

float sal;

};

struct emp e = {"John"};

printf ("%d %d", e.age , e.sal);
```

```
return 0;

}
```

Answer: 0 0.00000

When an automatic structure is partially initialized, the remaining elements of the structure are initialized to 0.

Q36. What will be the output of the below C program?

```
#include <stdio.h>

int main()

{

int a[5] = {1,2};

printf ("%d %d %d\n", a[2] , a[3] , a[4]);

return 0;

}
```

ANSWER: 0 0 0

When an automatic array is partially initialized, the remaining array elements are initialized to 0.

Q37. Which of the following structure declaration is incorrect?

1. struct aa

```
{

int a;

int b;

};
```

2. struct aa

```
{
int a;

float b;

struct aa var;

};
```

3. struct aa

```
{
int a;

float b;

struct aa *var;

};
```

4. struct aa

```
{
int a;

float b;

struct aa **var;

};
```

Answer: 2

The concept is that inside a structure declaration we can't declare a variable type of that structure. Since, during declaring a structure no memory is allocated. However we can create a pointer to same structure inside structure declaration. Such type of pointers, are called **self referential** pointer. (We will learn more on structure and its pointer in a separate chapter).

Q38. What is the output of following C code?

```c
typedef enum errorType {warning, error, exception,} error;
int main()
{
error g1;
g1=1;
printf ("%d", g1);

return 0;
}
```

Answer: Compile time error: 'Multiple declarations for error'.

The name error is used in the two meanings. One means that it is an enumerator constant with value 1. Another use is that it is a type name (due to typedef) for enum errorType. Given a situation the compiler cannot distinguish the meaning of error to know in what sense the error is used:

error g1;

g1= error;   // which error it refers in each case?

When the compiler can distinguish between usages then it will not issue error (in pure technical terms, names can only be overloaded in different namespaces).

Note: The extra comma in the declaration, enum errorType {warning, error, exception,} is not an error. An extra comma is valid and is provided just for programmer's convenience.

Q39. What will be the output of below C code?

```c
#include <stdio.h>

int main()

{

enum status {married, divorced, single};
```

```
enum status per1, per2, per3;

per1 = single;

per2 = married;

per3 = divorced;

printf ("%d %d %d", per1, per2, per3);

return 0;

}
```

ANSWER: 2 0 1

Explanation:

1. The first part declares the data type and specifies its possible values. These values are called 'enumerators'.

2. The second part declares variables of this data type.

Internally, the compiler treats the enumerators as integers. Each value on the list of permissible values corresponds to an integer, starting with 0. Thus in our example divorced is stored as 1, married is stored as 0 and single is stored as 2.

Q40. What will be the output of below C code?

```
#include <stdio.h>

int main()

{

union a

{

short int i;

char ch[2];
```

};

union a u;

u.ch[0] = 3;

u.ch[1] = 2;

printf ("%d %d %d\n" , u.ch[0], u.ch[1], u.i);

return 0;

}

ANSWER: Refer Chapter- 9 for better understanding.

Q41. What will be the output of below C program?

```
#include <stdio.h>

int main()

{
int x;

printf ("%d", scanf ("%d", &x));

/* suppose that input value for above scanf is 20 */

return 0;

}
```

ANSWER: 1

scanf () always return **int.** i,e it returns number of inputs it has successfully read.

Q42. What will be the output of below C code?

```
#include <stdio.h>

int main()
```

```
{
char a = '\012';

printf ("%d", a);

return 0;

}
```

ANSWER: 10

The value '\012' means the character with value 12 in octal which is decimal 10.

Chapter-2

Problems On Data Types

Q1. What is the range of different data types in C?

Answer:

Data Type	Range
1) signed char	-128 to +127
2) unsigned char	0 to 255
3) short signed int	-32768 to +32767
4) short unsigned int	0 to 65535
5) signed int	-32768 to +32767
6) unsigned int	0 to 65535
7) float	-3.4e8 to +3.4e38
8) double	-1.7e308 to +1.7e308
9) long double	-1.7e4932 to +1.7e4932

Note: - Range in this figure is for 16-bit compiler (Turbo C++)

There are also two data types- **long signed int** and **long unsigned int**. These two data type are rarely used.

Q2. What will be the output of following C program?

#include <stdio.h>

int main()

{

int i;

```
for (i = 0; i <= 50000; i++)

printf ("%d", i);

return 0;

}
```

Answer: Program will stuck-up into infinite loop.

Here variable **i** has been declared as **int** and on Turbo C/C++ compiler (16-bit) an integer can have values between -32768 to +32767. Hence, as value of **i** becomes greater than +32767, value of **i** becomes -32768 and thus value of **i** would keep oscillating between -32768 to +32767 thereby ensuring that loop never gets terminated.

Q3. What will be the output of below C program?

```
#include <stdio.h>

int main()

{

char ch = 291;

printf ("%d %c", ch, ch );

return 0;

}
```

Answer: 35 #

It should be 291 and the character corresponding to it. Well, not really. Surprised? The reason is that variable **ch** is of **char** type and a **char** cannot take value bigger than +127. Hence when value of **char** exceeds +127, an appropriate value from other side of the range is picked up and stored in **ch.** In our case it happens to be 35 and #.

Q4. What will be the output of below C program?

```c
#include <stdio.h>

int main()

{

static int var = 5;

printf ("%d\t", var--);

if (var != 0)

main ();

}
```

Answer: 5 4 3 2 1

Here, variable **var** is of type **int** but having **static** storage class. So, the value of **var** persists between the function calls (recursive call).

Q5. What will be the output of below C code?

```c
#include <stdio.h>

int x = 10;

int main()

{

int x =20;

{

int x = 30;

printf ("%d ", x);

}

printf ("%d ", x);

return 0;
```

}

Answer: 30 20

The output is obvious and storage class of variable is **auto.** Scope concept of a variable will work here.

Q6. What will be the output of below C program?

```
#include <stdio.h>

int main()

{

static int i = 5;

if (--i)

{

main();

printf ("%d ", i);

}

return 0;

}
```

ANSWER: 0 0 0 0

Since **i** is a static variable and is stored in Data Section (i, e having **static** storage class), all calls to main share same **i**. That is, value persists between different recursive calls.

Q7. What will be the output of below C code?

```
#include <stdio.h>

int main()
```

```
{
    unsigned int i=10;

    while (i-- >= 0)

    printf ("%u ",i);

    return 0;
}
```

ANSWER: The program goes into infinite loop.

9 8 7 6 5 4 3 2 1 0 4294967295 4294967294 ...... (On a machine where **int** is 4 bytes long)

9 8 7 6 5 4 3 2 1 0 65535 65534 .... (On a machine where **int** is 2 bytes long).

Here, variable **i** is an **unsigned int** and in **while** loop we are decrementing the value of **i**. But when the value becomes less than 0 then the roll-over happens and **i** takes the value of the highest +ve value, an **unsigned int** can take. So **i** will never negative. Therefore, it becomes infinite loop.

As a side note, if **i** was a **signed int**, the **while** loop would have been terminated after printing the highest negative value.

Q8. What will be the output of below C code?

```
#include <stdio.h>

int x;

void main()

{

printf ("%d", x);

}
```

ANSWER: 0

As explained in previous chapter, here variable **x** is having global scope and hence by default it holds zero.

Q9. What will be the output of below C program?

```c
#include <stdio.h>

int x = 5;

void main()

{

int x = 3;

printf ("%d ", x);

{

x = 4;

}

printf ("%d", x);

}
```

ANSWER: 3 4

Here we have declared two variables having same name but different scope namely global and local. **x** inside **main** () is **auto** and local. Then we have changed the value to 4 by creating another local scope. And again local gets priority over global one.

Think about the below one.

Q10. What will be the output of below C program?

```c
#include <stdio.h>

int x = 5;
```

```
void main()

{

int x = 3;

printf ("%d", x);

{

int x = 4;

}

printf ("%d ", x);

}
```

ANSWER: 3 3

Q11. What will be the output of below C code?

```
#include <stdio.h>

int main()

{

printf ("%d", d++);

return 0;

}

int d = 10;
```

ANSWER: Compile time error.

Here what we have done is that we have declared variable **d** outside **main** ()
and printing the value inside the **main** (). To make our program successfully
compile add this one before **printf** (): **extern int d;**

As mentioned in previous chapter **extern int d** is a declaration and definition has been done outside the **main** ().

Q12. What will be the output of below C program?

#include <stdio.h>

int main()

{

char *p;

printf ("%d %d ", sizeof(*p), sizeof(p));

return 0;

}

ANSWER: 1 2 (On a 16-bit compiler)

The **sizeof** () operator gives the number of bytes taken by its operand. **p** is a character pointer, which needs one byte for storing its value (a character). Hence **sizeof** (*p) gives a value of 1. Since it needs 2/4 bytes to store the address of the character pointer, **sizeof** (p) gives 2 or 4.

Q13. What will be output of the following C code?

#include<stdio.h>

int main()

{

signed x;

unsigned y;

x = 10 +- 10u + 10u +- 10;

y = x;

if (x == y)

printf ("%d %d", x, y);

else if (x != y)

printf ("%u %u", x, y);

return 0;

}

ANSWER: 0 0

Here, **x** is a signed integer variable, 10 is **signed** integer constant and 10u is unsigned integer constant. x = 10 +- 10u + 10u +- 10 in this expression we have different data types and we are performing binary operation.

Lower data type operand always automatically promoted into the operand of higher data type before performing the operation and result will be higher data type.

As we know operators enjoy higher precedence than binary operators. So our expression is:

x = 10 + (-10u) + 10u + (-10)

= 10u + -10u + 10u + -10u

= 0

Else is clear and simple to interpret.

Note: - **unsigned int** is higher data type than **signed int**. Hence corresponding **unsigned** value of signed 10 is **+10u**.

Q14. What will be the output of below C program?

#include <stdio.h>

int main()

{

float f1 = 0.1;

if (f1 == 0.1)

printf ("Equal");

else

printf ("Not equal")

return 0;

}

ANSWER: Not equal

In C by default data type of numeric constants is **double**. Hence 0.1 is of type **double**. **float** is never equal to **double**. Hence **else** block gets executed and hence the output.

Q15. What will be the output of below C program?
#include <stdio.h>

int main()

{

float f1 = 0.1;

if (f1 == 0.1f)

printf ("Equal");

else

printf ("Not equal");

return 0;

}

ANSWER: Equal

Q16. What will be the output of below C program?

```c
#include <stdio.h>

int main()

{

float x = 'a';

printf ("%f", x);

return 0;

}
```

ANSWER: 97.000000

Since the ASCII value of **a** is 97, the same is assigned to the **float** variable and hence printed.

Q17. What will be the output of below C code?

```c
#include <stdio.h>

int main()

{

float a = 0.5;

if (0.5 > a)

printf ("C");

else

printf ("C++");

return 0;

}
```

ANSWER: C

Here variable **a** is of **float** type and constant value 0.5 is of **double**. When we assign 0.5 to **a** then in memory 32-bit binary equivalent of 0.5 gets stored. And this binary equivalent value is a recurring number and gets terminated at 32 bits when it is stored in **a** whereas when 0.5 is treated as **double** then the same recurring binary equivalent of 0.5 is terminated at 64 bits. And it is obvious that 64-bit recurring binary equivalent of 0.5 is always greater than 32-bit recurring binary equivalent. Hence **if** condition gets true and hence the output.

Q18. What will be the output of below C program?

```c
#include <stdio.h>

union un

{

int num;

char m;

};

int main()

{

union un s;

printf ("%d", sizeof(s));

return 0;

}
```

ANSWER: 2 bytes (16-bit compiler)

4 bytes (32-bit compiler)

Since the size of a union variable is the size of its maximum data type. Here **int** is the largest, hence 2 or 4 depending on your compiler type.

Q19. What will be the output of below C program?

```c
#include <stdio.h>
int main()
{
register int x = 0;
if (x < 2)
{
x++;
main();
}
return 0;
}
```

ANSWER: Error- "Segmentation fault".

We can't access register variables. It is used by compiler internally.

Q20. What will be the default data type of following declaration?

(i)   short i=10;

(ii)   static i=10;

(iii)   unsigned i=10;

(iv)   const i=10;

ANSWER: **int**

Q21. What will be output when you will execute following c code?

```c
#include<stdio.h>
```

```
int main()

{

int a = sizeof(signed) + sizeof(unsigned);

int b = sizeof(const) + sizeof(volatile);

printf ("%d", a++ + b);
return 0;

}
```

ANSWER: 8 (16-bit compiler) and 16 (32-bit compiler)

Default data type of **signed, unsigned, const** and **volatile** is **int**.

Q22. What is the output of this C code?

```
#include <stdio.h>

union

{

int x;

char y;

}p;

int main()

{

p.x = 10;

printf ("%d", sizeof(p));

}
```

ANSWER: **sizeof (int)** i, e 2 or 4 bytes depending on your compiler.

Q23. Will the below C program compile successfully?

```c
#include <stdio.h>

int main()

{

float i =5, *j;

void *k;

k = &i;

j = k;

printf ("%d",*j);

return 0;

}
```

ANSWER: Yes, program will compile.

In C one can assign the one data type to and from **k** in this case. No typecasting is required here. Conversions are done automatically by compiler when other pointer types are assigned to and from **void *;**

Q24. Will following C program successfully compile?

```c
#include <stdio.h>

int main()

{

int x = 5, *j;

void *k;

j = k = &x;

j++;

++k;
```

printf ("%d %d", *j, *k);

return 0;

}

ANSWER: No, program will not compile. Rule says we can't perform arithmetic operations on **void** pointers.

Q25. Which of the following is integral data type?

    1) void

    2) char

    3) float

    4) double

    5) long double

ANSWER: char

In C, char is integral data type. It stores the ASCII value of any character constant.

Q26. What will be output of following C code?

```
#include <stdio.h>

int main()

{

signed x, a;

unsigned y, b;

a = (signed) 10u;

b = (unsigned) -10;

y = (signed) 10u + (unsigned) -10;
```

```
x = y;

printf ("%d  %u\t", a, b);

if (x==y)

printf ("%d %d", x, y);

else if (x!=y)

printf("%u  %u", x, y);

return 0;

}
```

ANSWER: 10 65526 0 0 (16-bit compiler)

   10 4294967286 0 0 (32-bit compiler)

Here signed value of 10u is +10 hence a = 10 but for b = (unsigned) -10

unsigned value of -10 is MAX_VALUE_OF_UNSIGNED_INT – 10 +1.

Hence for Turbo C/C++, max value of **unsigned int** is 65535. Hence b = 65535. Now below expression is like:

y = (signed) 10u + (unsigned) -10;

   = 10 + 65526 = 65536

But 65536 is beyond the range of Turbo C/C++ compiler and also variable **y** is of **unsigned** type. So, roll over happens and 0 is taken.

Range of **unsigned int** is: 0 - 65535

Q27. What will be the output of following C code?

```
#include<stdio.h>

int main()

{
```

```
int a = -5;

unsigned int b = -5u;

if (a == b)

printf ("Hello");

else

printf ("Hi");

return 0;

}
```

ANSWER: Hello

Here, int a = -5; variable "*a*" is by default signed int and its corresponding unsigned int value will be:

$65535 - 5 + 1 = 65531$

So, a = 65531

In any binary operation of dissimilar data type for example: a == b

Lower data type operand always automatically type casted into the operand of higher data type before performing the operation and result will be higher data type.

In C **unsigned int** is higher data type than **signed int**. So, variable **a** will be automatically gets promoted into **unsigned int**.

So, corresponding signed value of 65531 is -5.

Q28. What will be the output of below C code?

```
#include <stdio.h>

int main()

{
```

```c
double num=5.2;

int var = 5;

printf ("%d\t ", sizeof(num));

printf ("%d\t ", sizeof(var = 15/2));

printf ("%d", var);
return 0;

}
```

ANSWER: 8 2 5 (16-bit compiler)

Note: - Expression is not evaluated inside the **sizeof** operator.

Q29. What will be the output of below C program?

```c
#include <stdio.h>

int main()

{
int i = 5;

printf ("%d ", sizeof(i++));

printf ("%d", i);

return 0;

}
```

ANSWER: 2(16-bit compiler) /4 (32-bit compiler) 5

Note: - **sizeof** operator only returns the memory occupied by any variable. Expressions are not evaluated inside sizeof.

Q30. What will be the output of below C code?

```c
#include <stdio.h>
```

```c
int initializer()

{

return 50;

}

int main()

{

static int i = initializer();

printf ("value of i = %d", i);

return 0;

}
```

ANSWER: Compile time error. In C, **static** variables can only be initialized using constant literals.

The reason for this is simple: All objects with static storage duration must be initialized (set to their initial values) before execution of **main** () starts. So a value which is not known at translation time cannot be used for initialization of **static** variables.

Q31. What will be the output of below C code?

```c
#include <stdio.h>

int main()

{

unsigned int x = -1;

int y = ~0;

if (x == y)

printf ("same");
```

else

printf ("not same");

return 0;

}

ANSWER: same

-1 and ~0 essentially have same bit pattern, hence **x** and **y** must be same. In the comparison, **y** is promoted to unsigned and compared against variable **x**. The result is "same". However, when interpreted as signed and unsigned their numerical values will differ. **x** is MAXUNIT and **y** is -1. Since we have **%u** for **y** also, the output will be MAXUNIT and MAXUNIT.

Q32. What will be the output of below C code?

```c
#include <stdio.h>

int main()

{

unsigned int a = 6;

int b = -20;

if (a+b > 6)

printf ("> 6")

else

puts ("<= 6");

return 0;

}
```

ANSWER: >6

The reason for this is that expressions involving **signed** and **unsigned** types have all operands promoted to **unsigned** types. Thus -20 becomes a very large positive integer and the expression evaluates to greater than 6.

Q33. What will be the output of below C code?

```c
#include <stdio.h>

int main()
{
int x = 2;

static int y = x;

if (x == y)

printf ("C");

else if (x > y)

printf ("C++");

else

printf ("Java");

return 0;

}
```

ANSWER: Compile time error. Refer Q.30 for explanation.

Chapter-3

Control Structures

Q1. What will be the output of following C program?

```c
#include <stdio.h>

int main()

{

int a = 500, b, c;

if (a >= 400)

  b = 100;

  c = 200;

printf ("%d %d", b, c);

return 0;

}
```

Answer: 100 GARBAGE VALUE

In this program, first **if** condition is checked and as value of variable **a** is greater than 400, so statement just below if executes i, e variable **b** is assigned 100.

Note: - The default scope of if statement is immediately after it. So 200 is not assigned to the variable **c.**

To actually assign the value in **c,** the statements after, **if** condition must be enclosed in a pair of braces.

Q2. What will be the output of the below C program?

```c
#include <stdio.h>

int main()

{
char ch;
if (ch = printf(""))
printf ("It matters. \n");
else
printf ("It does not matter. \n");
return 0;

}
```

Answer: It does not matter.

Inside **if** statement 0 is assigned to variable **ch** because printf prints nothing on console hence it returns 0 and hence **if** condition evaluates to false. Thereby making **else** block to execute.

Note: - In C a non-zero value is considered to be **true**, whereas a 0 is considered to be **false**.

Q3. What will be the output of following C program?

```c
#include <stdio.h>

int main()

{
if (sizeof(void))
printf ("C");
```

else

printf ("Java");

return 0;

}

Answer: Compilation Error- "Not an allowed type in function main".

It is illegal to find size of **void** data type using **sizeof** operator. It is because **sizeof** for **void** data type is undefined.

Q4. What will be the output of following C program?

```
#include <stdio.h>
int main()
{
int i = 3;
switch(i)
{
default: printf ("zero");
case 1: printf ("one");
break;
case 2: printf ("two");
break;
case 3: printf ("three");
break;
}
}
```

Answer: three

The **default case** can be placed anywhere inside the loop. It is executed only when all other cases doesn't match.

Q5. What will be the output of following C code?

```c
#include <stdio.h>

int main()

{
int i = 4;
switch(i)
{
default: printf("zero");
case 1:  printf("one");
break;
case 2:  printf("two");
break;
case 3:  printf("three");
break;
}

}
```

ANSWER : zeroone

Q6. What will be the output of following C program?

```c
#include <stdio.h>

const int a = 1, b = 2;

int main()

{
int x = 1;

switch (x)

{

case a:
```

```
printf("Yes");

case b:

printf("No");

break;

}

return 0;

}
```

ANSWER: Compile time error.

The structure of switch-case –default appears as:

```
switch (constant expression)

{

case constant 1:

do this;

case constant 2:

do this;

case constant 3:

do this;

default :

do this finally;

}
```

The integer expression following the keyword switch is any C expression that evaluates to an integer value. It could be an integer constant like 1, 2, and 3 etc. or an expression that results into an integer constant.

Each constant in each **case** must be different from each other. Any valid constant expression can be in **case**. Variables are not allowed in **case**.

Note: - The keyword **case** is followed by an integer or a character constant only.

Q7. What will be the output of below C program?

```
#include <stdio.h>

#define max(a) a

int main()
{
int x = 1;

switch (x)
{
 case max(2):
printf("Yes");

case max(1):
printf("No");

break;

}
return 0;

}
```

ANSWER: No

Here program works fine because macros are processed before compile time i, e during preprocessing hence max (2) and max (1) are replaced by constant integer values.

Q8. What will be output of following C program?

```c
#include <stdio.h>
int main()
{
switch (printf("Do"))
{
case 1:
printf ("First\n");
break;
case 2:
printf ("Second\n");
break;
default:
printf ("Default");
break;
}
}
```

ANSWER: DoSecond

Here printf inside **switch** return 2 which is of integer type and **case** corresponding to this **switch** gets executed.

Q9. What do you think about following C code? What should be printed on the console?

```c
#include <stdio.h>
int main()
```

```
{
int a = 10;

switch(a)

{
case '1':

        printf ("ONE\n");

case '2':

        printf ("TWO\n");

defa1ut:

        printf ("NONE");

}

return 0;

}
```

ANSWER: You must be thinking that NONE will be printed but nothing will be printed. Check **default** has been correctly written or not. Last line acts as a label only.

Q10. What will be the output of following C code?

```
#include <stdio.h>

#define L 10

int main()

{
auto i =10;

switch(i , i*2);
```

```
{
case L:  printf ("C");
        break;
case L*2: printf ("C++");
        break;
case L*3: printf ("Java");
        break;
default: printf ("Perl");
case L*4: printf ("Ruby");
        break;
}
return 0;
}
```

ANSWER: C++

In this program main thing is to observe is comma (,) operator inside switch. **comma** operator enjoy least precedence. Hence if we have:

a = (x , y);

then a = y

not x

Note: Case expression can be a macro constant.

Q11. What will be output when you will execute following C code?

```
#include<stdio.h>
int main()
```

```c
{
const char *str="ONE"

str++;

switch(str)

{
case "ONE":

printf ("Brazil");

break;

case "NE":

printf ("USA");

break;

case "N":

printf ("Canada");

break;

case "E":

printf ("Spain");

}
return 0;

}
```

ANSWER: Compile time error.

case expression cannot be a **string** constant.

Q12. What will be the output of following C program?

```c
#include <stdio.h>

int main()
{
int a = 2;
switch(a)
{
printf ("Hello");
case 1:
printf ("C");
break;
case 2:
printf ("C++");
break;
}
return 0;
}
```

ANSWER: C++

Every statement in a **switch** must belong to some **case** or other. If a statement doesn't belong to any **case,** the compiler won't report an error. However the statement would never get executed.

Hence first **printf** () will not execute.

Q13. What will be output when you will execute following c code?

#include <stdio.h>

```c
void main()
{
switch(6)
{
case 6.0f:
    printf ("India");
    break;
case 6.0:
    printf ("Pakistan");
    break;
case 6.0L:
    printf ("Sri Lanka");
    break;
default:  printf ("Nepal");
}
}
```

ANSWER: Error: case label does not reduce to an integer constant

In C, **switch** expression must return an integer value. It cannot be **float, double** or **long double**.

Q14. What will be the output of following C code?

```c
#include <stdio.h>

int main()
{
```

```
switch(0X0)

{

case NULL:  printf ("C");

            break;

case '\0': printf ("C++");

        break;

case 0: printf ("Java");

        break;

default: printf (".Net");

}

return 0;

}
```

ANSWER: Compile time error.

In C duplicate **case** is not allowed. Here, **0x0** is actually in **hex** and its decimal value is 0 and also macro **NULL** is nothing but 0, defined in stddef.h or stdio.h header file. ASCII value of character constant '\0' is 0. Hence duplicate **case** is there in our code.

Q15. What will be the output of following C program?

```
#include <stdio.h>

enum country = { India = 4, Nepal = 5, Bhutan = -1, Sri Lanka};

int main()

{

enum country e = 0;
```

```
switch(e)

{

case India : printf ("Hello India");

        break;

case Nepal : printf ("Hello Nepal");

        break;

case Bhutan : printf ("Hello Bhutan");

        break;

case Sri Lanka : printf ("Hello Sri Lanka");

        break;

}

return 0;

}
```

ANSWER: Hello Sri Lanka

In C we can have **enum** constant in **case.** Internally compiler treats the enumerators as integers. Each value on the list of permissible values corresponds to an integer starting with 0. But in our case India is stored as 4 and so on. Sri Lanka gets stored as 0 because Bhutan is before Sri Lanka and its value is -1 hence for Sri Lanka value is (-1 + 1) i,e 0.

Q16. What will be the output of below C code?

```
#include <stdio.h>

int main()

{

int x = 20;
```

```c
int a[] = {10, 20, 30};

switch (x)

{

case a[0]: printf ("C");

case a[1]: printf ("C++");

case a[2]: printf ("Java");

}

return 0;

}
```

ANSWER: Compile time error.

case labels must be integer constant inside **switch** block.

Q17. Can there be a switch without any cases?

ANSWER: Yes, we can have a switch without any case.

Take a look at below C code.

```c
#include <stdio.h>

int main()

{

int i = 5;

switch( i )

{

}

printf ("We can have a switch without any case\n");
```

```c
return 0;
}
```

Q18. What will be the output of below C code?

```c
#include <stdio.h>

int main()
{
int a = 0;
while (a++ != 0 )
printf ("%d ", ++a);
printf ("\n");
return 0;
}
```

ANSWER: Nothing will be printed on the console.

Here reason behind printing nothing is clear.Every time **while** loop gets false.

Q19. What will be the output of following C program?

```c
#include <stdio.h>

int main()
{
int a = 2 , b =2;
while (a+1 ? --a : b++)
printf ("%d", a);
return 0;
```

}

ANSWER: 1

Here in this program, we have **ternary operator** inside **while** loop.

Ternary operator has following format:

<condition> ? <true-case-code>: <false-case-code>

The ternary operator allows you to execute different code depending on the value of a condition, and the result of the expression is the result of the executed code. So if, <condition> gets true then <true-case-code> will be executed otherwise <false-case-code> will be executed.

a + 1 will be 3(true in C/C++) hence **--a** get executed. So **a** now becomes 1 not 2. Think why? And thus **while** loop gets true and it prints 1.

Note:-Before solving problems on for loop and while loop. Let's go through the general syntax of both.

/* for loop*/

for (<init-stmnt>; <boolean-expr>; <incr-stmnt>)

{

  <body-statements>

}

 /* While loop*/

<init-stmnt>;

while (<boolean-expr>)

{

  <body-statements>

  <incr-stmnt>

}

Q20. What will be the output of following C code?

```
#include <stdio.h>

int main()

{

static int k;

for (++k; ++k; ++k)

{

printf ("%d ", k);

if (k == 4)

break;

}

return 0;

}
```

ANSWER: 2   4

Variable **a**, has **static** storage class so default value of **a** will be zero.

Q21. Will the following C program successfully? If not, why?

```
#include<stdio.h>

int main()

{

int i = 10;

int c = 10;
```

```c
switch (c)

{

case i:

printf ("Value of c = %d", c);

break;

/* Some more cases */

}

return 0;

}
```

ANSWER: No, In C switch statement, the expression of each **case** label must be an integer constant expression.

Think about the below one.

Q22. Will the following C program work fine? Why?

```c
#include<stdio.h>

int main()

{

const int i = 10;

int c = 10;

switch(c)

{

case i:

printf ("Value of c = %d", c);

break;
```

```
/* Some more cases */

}

return 0;

}
```

ANSWER: No, never. **switch** statement is used in lieu of large if-else ladder when an identifier is compared against a set of integral constants. switch is another alternative that follows a table loop-up approach in determining correct if-else clause. The compiler makes read-only switch case 'constants table' in non-decreasing order and invokes binary search on the table to determine exact case statement. It improves performance a lot. Due to this fact, most of the compilers place the switch tables in read-only memory. An attempt to modify such case integral value can result in runtime error. It is suggested only integral constants (integers, enumerated constants, macros, etc.) to be used as case labels.

Q23. What will be the output of below C code?

```
#include <stdio.h>

int main()

{

int i;

for (i = -1; i<= 10; i++)

{

if(i < 5)

continue;

else

break;
```

printf ("Concepts In C");

}

return 0;

}

ANSWER: Nothing will be printed on console.

Here until variable i don't become equal to or more than 5 continue works. But as soon as i becomes 5 if () gets false and hence else block gets executed. break takes out the control from the that for () loop in which it is placed. In this case we have only one for () loop hence printf () never gets executed.

Note: - **break** statement terminates any type of loop like **while** loop, **do while** loop and **for** loop. **break** statement terminates the loop body immediately and passes control to the next statement after the loop.

continue statement skips the rest of the current iteration in a loop and returns to the top of the loop.

Q24. What will be the output of below C code?

```
#include <stdio.h>

int main()

{

int i = 0;

for(i = 0; i <= 127; printf ("%d", i++))

;

printf ("\n");

return 0;

}
```

ANSWER: 0 1 2 3 ....125 126 127

Output is obvious. In C, ";" is an executable statement and hence it doesn't cause any error. Remember the note given below Q18. I have replaced <incr-stmnt> with **printf** ("%d", i++). Others are same. Try to think the rest of the working at your own.

Q25. What will be the output of below C code?

```c
#include <stdio.h>

int main()

{

int i = 1;

for (i = 2; i=-1; i = 1)

{

printf ("%d", i);

if (i != 1)

break;

}

return 0;

}
```

ANSWER: -1

Think again. Simple one just go through **for** () loop syntax.

Q26. What will be the output of following C code?

```c
#include <stdio.h>

int main()
```

```c
{
int num = 1;

while (num < 20)

{
if (num % 3 == 1)

printf ("Number = %d\n", num);

num += 2;

}
return 0;

}
```

ANSWER: Number = 1

Number = 7

Number = 13

Number = 19

% is **modulus** operator in C. It always gives remainder. Hence whenever remainder is equal to 1, **printf** () gets executed. **num += 2** is not part of **if** block. So num += 2 is executed till **while** loop is true.

Q27. What will the output of below C code?

```c
#include <stdio.h>

int main()

{
for (; ;)

{
```

```c
printf ("Hello World");

}

return 0;

}
```

ANSWER: It's an infinite loop. The program will keep on printing Hello World until the stack overflows. Remember an infinite loop (sometimes called an endless loop) is a piece of coding that lacks a functional exit so that it repeats indefinitely.

Let's see some different ways of infinite loop in C.

1. **Semicolon at end of while loop**.
   ```c
   #include <stdio.h>
   int main()
   {
   int num = 300;
   while(num > 255);  // Note carefully here. Semicolon at end of
   {                  // while loop means loop without any body.
   printf("Hello");
   num--;
   }
   ```
2. **Non-Zero Number as a parameter**.
   ```c
   #include <stdio.h>
   int main()
   {
   while (1)   // A non-zero is given inside loop so loop will always be
   {           // TRUE and this condition is not changing.
   printf("Hello C");
   }
   return 0;
   }
   ```
3. **Subscript variable remains the same**.

```
#include <stdio.h>
int main()
{
int num = 20;
while(num > 10)  // condition is mentioned but terminating condition
{                      // is not mentioned i, e subscript is neither
printf("Concepts In C");    // incremented or decremented.
}
}
```

There may be many ways of having infinite loop.

Q28. What will be the output of below C code?

```
#include <stdio.h>

int main()

{

int i = 0;

for (; i < 5; i++);

printf ("%d ", i);

return 0;

}
```

ANSWER: 5

Reason is simple. Carefully watch **for** loop. It is terminated by **;** (semi colon).

Q29. What will be the output of below C code?

```
#include <stdio.h>

int main()

{
```

char ch = 125;

do

{

printf ("%d ", ch);

}while (ch++);

return 0;

}

ANSWER: 125 126 127 -128 -127 -126 .... -4 -3 -2 -1 0

Note: - The following illustrates the syntax of the do while loop statement:

do

{

// execution statements

} while (expression);   // here expression evaluates to Boolean value.

The **do while** loop statement consists of execute statements and a Boolean condition. First the execute statements are executed, and then the condition is checked. If the condition evaluates to true, the execute statements are executed again until the condition evaluates to false.

Q30. What will be the output of below C code?

#include <stdio.h>

int main()

{

int i = 321;

int val = printf ("Hello C");

```
for (i = 0; i <= val; i++)

printf ("%d ", i);

return 0;

}
```

ANSWER: Hello C 0 1 2 3 4 5 6 7

Reason is obvious. Here **printf** () returns 7 and **for** loop executes for this much time to give desired output.

Q31. What will be the output of below C code?

```
#include <stdio.h>

int main()

{

int a = 1, b = 1;

for (; b; printf ("%d %d\n", a,b))

  b = a++ <= 5;

return 0;

}
```

ANSWER: 2 1

       3 1

       4 1

       5 1

       6 1

       7 0

Here firstly value of variable **a** will be compared against 5 and if it is true then 1 will be assigned to variable **b** but before assignment the value of **a** will be incremented (postfix expression). Rest of the things are simple and obvious.

Q32. What will be the output of below C code?

#include <stdio.h>

int main()

{

int n;

for (n = 7; n != 0; n--)

printf ("n = %d", n--);

return 0;

}

ANSWER: Above program goes in infinite loop because **n** is never zero when loop condition (**n != 0**) is checked.

Try this one at your own.

Q33. What will be the output of following C code?

#include <stdio.h>

int main()

{

char ch = 0;

for (ch <= 5 && ch>= -1; ++ch; ch > 0)

printf ("%d ", ch);

printf ("\n");

return 0;

}

ANSWER: 1 2 3 4 5 6 ....125 126 127 ...... -9 -8 -7..... -2 -1

Q34. What will be the output of below C code?

```c
#include <stdio.h>

enum {false, true};

int main()
{
int i = 1;

do
{
printf("%d ", i);
i++;


if (i < 15)
continue;
} while (false);

return 0;
}
```

ANSWER: 1

The **do while** loop, checks condition after each iteration. So after **continue** statement, control transfers to the statement **while** (false). Since the condition is false 'i' is printed only once. I think most of you are now clear with the working concept of **do while** loop. Try below one now.

Q35. What will be the output of below C code?

#include <stdio.h>

enum {false, true};

int main()

{

int i = 1;

do

{

printf ("%d ", i);

i++;

if (i < 15)

break;

} while (true);

return 0;

}

ANSWER: 1

Did you notice on **enum**? Try changing the position of true and false. See what's happen? It is an important concept of **enum** in C.

Q36. Find the error in below C code?

#include <stdio.h>

int main()

```c
{
int x = 5, num = 1000;

do

{

num /= x;

} while(x--)

printf ("%d ", num);

return 0;

}
```

ANSWER: Runtime Error. Can't divide by zero. Watch carefully. Debug the code, you will find.

Q37. What will be the output of below C code?

```c
#include <stdio.h>

int main()

{

int i, j;

i = j = 4, 5;

while (--i && j++)

{

printf ("%d %d", i, j);

printf ("\n");

}

return 0;
```

}

ANSWER: 3 5

      2 6

      1 7

Initial value of variable: - i = 4, j = 5

Consider the while condition: --i && j++

In first iteration: --i && j++

= 3 && 5 //In C any non-zero number represents true.

= 1 (True)

So **while** loop condition is true. Hence **printf** () will print value of i = 3 and j = 5 (Due to post increment operator). And in the same way program executes until **while** loop doesn't get false.

Q38. How many times will the loop bodies execute in the following loops?

```c
#include <stdio.h>
int main()
{
int x = 4, y = 50;
do
{
x += 8;
printf ("Hello %d\n", C);
} while (x < y);
return 0;
```

}

ANSWER: 6 times. Think.

Q39. What will be the output of below C code?

#include <stdio.h>

int main()

{

int x = 001, i;

for (i = 0; i < x; i+=3)

{

printf ("Hello World");

continue;

printf ("Bye");

}

return 0;

}

ANSWER: Hello World Hello World Hello World

011 is octal number. Its equivalent decimal value is 9. Hence x = 9

First iteration: i = 0

i < x i, e 0 < 9 i, e loop condition is true. Hence printf statement will print: Hello World. Due to **continue** keyword program control will come at the beginning of for loop and value of variable **i** will be: i += 3 i, e i = i + 3 = 3. Second iteration: i = 3

i < x i, e 3 < 9 and hence loop condition is true.

Hence again **printf** statement will print: Hello World

And this way program executes until **for** loop don't become false.

Q40. What will be the output of below C code?

```c
#include <stdio.h>

enum {false, true};

extern int a;

int main()
{
do
{
    do
    {
        printf ("%o", a);
    } while (! 1);
} while (false);

return 0;
}
int a = 10;
```

ANSWER: 12

Here we have nested **do while** loop. As we know do while executes at least one time even that condition is false. Here variable **a**, is of **extern** type. So it will search the definition of variable **a**, which is present at the end of the code. So value of variable **a**, is 8. In C, **%o** is used to print the number in octal format. So, octal value of variable **a**, is 12.

Q41. What will be the output of below C code?

```c
#include <stdio.h>

int main()

{

if (! printf("Chandra Prakash"))

if (printf("Author"));

return 0;

}
```

ANSWER: Chandra Prakash

The above program will not print Author because first **printf** will print Chandra Prakash first and then it will return 15. But after negation 15 becomes 0 and hence first **if** becomes false and due to this second **printf** doesn't get executed.

Q42. What will be output of following C code?

```c
#include <stdio.h>

int main()

{

int x = 4;

if (printf("%d", x<=4) – 5)

{

for (;;)

{

break;
```

}

}

else;

return 0;

}

ANSWER: 1

<= is an operator in C which returns 1 if true or 0 if false. But here it will return 1 and hence printf will print 1 on console. Next we will have -4 inside **if** which is again a true value in C. So, **if** block will be executed but for (;;) is an infinite loop and break will simply take out the control out of this infinite loop. So our program will not go into an infinite loop.

Q43. What will be the output of below C code?

```c
#include <stdio.h>

int main()
{
char ch = 'a';

switch (ch)
{
case 'a' || 1: printf ("C");

case 'b' || 2: printf ("C++");

break;

default: printf ("Perl");
}

return 0;
```

}

ANSWER: Compile time error.

The expressions used in each **case** label are evaluated to true i, e 1 and hence we have duplicate **case** value which results into compile time error.

Q44. What will be the output of below C code?

```c
#include <stdio.h>

int main()

{

unsigned int i = 1;

for (; i > -2; --i)

printf ("Concepts In C");

return 0;

}
```

ANSWER: Nothing will be printed.

Variable **i,** is of **unsigned** type and when compared with **signed** type, the **signed** value automatically gets promoted to **unsigned** type. Hence, -2 will become a huge number and thus loop gets false and control comes out of **for** () loop and nothing gets printed on console.

Q45. What will be the output of below C code?

```c
#include <stdio.h>

int main()

{

unsigned int i = 3;

if (i > -1)
```

```
printf ("Hell");

else

printf ("Heaven");

}
```

ANSWER: Heaven

Chapter-4

Expressions In C

Q1. What will be the output of below C code?

```
#include <stdio.h>

int main()

{

int i = -1, j = -1, k = 0, l = 2, m;

m = i++ && j++ && k++ || l++;

printf ("%d %d %d %d %d\n", i, j, k, l, m);

return 0;

}
```

ANSWER: 0 0 1 3 1

Logical operations always give a result of 1 or 0. And also the logical AND (&&) operator has higher priority over the logical OR (||) operator. So the expression 'i++ && j++ && k++' is executed first. The result of this expression is 0 (-1 && -1 && 0 = 0). Now the expression is 0 || 2 which evaluates to 1 (because OR operator always gives 1 except for '0 || 0' combination- for which it gives 0). So the value of m is 1. The values of other variables are also incremented by 1.

Q2. What will be the output of below C code?

```
#include <stdio.h>

int main()

{

int i = 5;
```

printf ("%d %d %d %d %d\n", i++, i--, ++i, --i, i);

return 0;

}

ANSWER: The perfect answer of such types of question should be- "Output will vary compiler to compiler". Let's see the output of this question on some popular compiler:-

Dev C++:   4 5 5 4 5

Reason: - The arguments in a function call are pushed into the stack from left to right. The evaluation is by popping out from the stack and the evaluation is from right to left, hence the result.

Ideone & codepad: 4 5 5 5 5

Here, different output. It is because these compilers are evaluating the arguments in a different ways not like Dev C++ so perfect answer is what I have mentioned at the beginning. It's up to the compiler you are using.

Q3. What will be the output of below C code?

#include <stdio.h>

int main()

{

int i = 5;

printf ("%d", i++ + ++i);

return 0;

}

ANSWER: 12 (Same on Dev C++, Ideone and codepad)

But, answer should be - Output will vary compiler to compiler.

Q4. What will be the output of below C code?

```c
#include <stdio.h>
int main()
{
int a = 3;
int b = ++a + a++ + --a;
printf ("%d", b);
return 0;
}
```

ANSWER: Output will vary compiler to compiler.

Q5. What will be the output below C code?

```c
#include <stdio.h>
int main()
{
int i = 5;
printf ("%d", i+++++i);
return 0;
}
```

ANSWER: Compile time error

The expression i+++++i is parsed as i ++ ++ + i which is an illegal combination of operators.

Q6. What will be the output of below C code?

```c
#include <stdio.h>
int main()
{
int i = -2, j = 3, k = 0, m;
m = ++i || ++j && ++k;
printf ("%d %d %d %d\n", m, k, j, i);
return 0;
}
```

ANSWER: 1 0 3 -1

Output is obvious. Explanation is same as given in Q1.

Q7. What will be the output of below C code?

```c
#include <stdio.h>
int main()
{
int i = -2, j = 3, k = 0, m;
m = ++i && ++j && ++k;
printf ("%d %d %d %d\n", i, j, k, m);
return 0;
}
```

ANSWER: -1 4 1 1

Note: - Remember the table given below for solving further problems.

Operators	Associativity
() [] -> .	left to right
! ~ ++ -- + - * (*type*) **sizeof**	right to left
* / %	left to right
+ -	left to right
<< >>	left to right
< <= > >=	left to right
== !=	left to right
&	left to right
^	left to right
|	left to right
&&	left to right
||	left to right
?:	right to left
= += -= *= /= %= &= ^= |= <<= >>=	right to left
, (comma operator)	left to right

Table: Precedence and Associativity of Operators

Q8. What will be the output of below C code?

```c
#include <stdio.h>

int main()

{

int i = 3, j;

j = i + (1, 2, 3, 4, 5);

printf ("%d", j);

return 0;
```

}

ANSWER: 8

In this question comma operator has been used. The comma operator has left to right associativity. The left operand is always evaluated first, and the result of evaluation is discarded before the right operand is evaluated. In this expression 5 is the right-most operand, hence after evaluating expression (1, 2, 3, 4, 5) the final result is 5, which on adding to i results into 8.

Q9. What will be the output of below C code?

#include <stdio.h>

int main()

{

int a, b, c, d;

a = 3;

b = 4;

c = a, b;

d = (a, b);

printf ("%d ", c);

printf ("%d ", d);

return 0;

}

ANSWER: 3 4

The comma operator evaluates both of its operands and produces the value of the second. It also has lower precedence than assignment. Hence c = a, b is equivalent to c = a, while d = (a, b) is equivalent to d = b.

Q10. What will be the output of below C code?

```c
#include <stdio.h>
int main()
{
int x = 10, y =20;
x = !x;
y = !x && !y;
printf ("x = %d  y = %d", x, y);
return 0;
}
```

ANSWER: x = 0 y = 0

Logical NOT operator has higher precedence than logical AND operator. ! will first invert variables x and y both and then logical && will operate.

Q11. What will be the output of below C code?

```c
#include <stdio.h>
int main()
{
int i = 5;
if ( (((++i < 6) && (i++/5)) || (++i <= 8));
printf ("i = %d\n", i);
return 0;
}
```

ANSWER: 7

Q12. What will be the output of below C code?

```c
#include <stdio.h>

int main()

{
int x = 10, y = 5, z;

z = x != 4 || y == 2;

printf ("z = %d\n", z);

return 0;

}
```

ANSWER: z = 1

!= operator has higher precedence than == operator. As x is 10 so x != 4 is true and hence it will return 1. Also left operand of || operator evaluates to true i, e 1 hence the operand, right to || operator will not evaluated.

Q13. What will be the output of below C code?

```c
#include <stdio.h>

int main()

{
int i = 44;

printf ("%d %d %d\n", i <= 44, i = 50, i >= 20);

return 0;

}
```

ANSWER: 1 50 1

Q14. What will be the output of below C code?

```c
#include <stdio.h>
int main()
{
int a, b, c, x;
a = b = c = 1;
x = ++a || ++b && ++c;
printf ("%d %d %d %d\n", x, a, b, c);
return 0;
}
```

ANSWER: 1 2 1 1

Q15. What is comma operator in C?

ANSWER: - Allows grouping two statements where one is expected.

expression, expression

The comma operator has left-to-right associativity. Two expressions separated by a comma are evaluated left to right. The left operand is always evaluated, and all side effects are completed before the right operand is evaluated.

Commas can be used as separators in some contexts, such as function argument lists. Do not confuse the use of the comma as a separator with its use as an operator; the two uses are completely different.

Consider the expression: e1, e2

The type and value of the expression are the type and value of e2; the result of evaluating e1 is discarded. The result is an l-value if the right operand is an l-value.

Where the comma is normally used as a separator (for example in actual arguments to functions or aggregate initializer), the comma operator and its operands must be enclosed in parentheses. For example:

func_one(x, y + 2, z);

func_two ((x--, y + 2), z);

In the function call to func_one above, three arguments, separated by commas, are passed: x, y + 2, and z. In the function call to func_two, parentheses force the compiler to interpret the first comma as the sequential-evaluation operator. This function call passes two arguments to func_two. The first argument is the result of the sequential-evaluation operation (x--, y + 2), which has the value and type of the expression y + 2; the second argument is z.

Q16. What will be the output of below C code?

```
#include <stdio.h>

int main()

{

int m, n;

int x = 0, y = 2;

for (m = 0, n = 0; m < x, n < y; m++, n++)

{

printf ("Concepts In C ");

}

return 0;

}
```

ANSWER: Concepts In C Concepts In C

The important thing is here to notice is expression (m < x, n < y), comma operator is separating the two sub expression. We know that when two expressions are separated by comma operator, the first expression (m < x) is executed first. Result of the first expression is ignored. Then the second expression (n < y) is executed and the result of this second expression is the final result of the complete expression (m < x, n < y). Now, sub expression n < y is true for two times and hence "Concepts In C" is printed two times on the console.

Q17. What is a sequence point in C?

ANSWER: A sequence point defines any point in a computer program's execution at which it is guaranteed that all side effects of previous evaluations will have been performed, and no side effects from subsequent evaluations have yet been performed.

Sequence points in C:

In C and C++ sequence points occur in the following places:

Between consecutive "sequence points" an object's value can be modified only once by an expression. The C language defines the following sequence points:

- Left operand of the logical-AND operator (**&&**). The left operand of the logical-AND operator is completely evaluated and all side effects complete before continuing. If the left operand evaluates to false (0), the other operand is not evaluated.

- Left operand of the logical-OR operator (||). The left operand of the logical-OR operator is completely evaluated and all side effects complete before continuing. If the left operand evaluates to true (nonzero), the other operand is not evaluated.

- Left operand of the comma operator. The left operand of the comma operator is completely evaluated and all side effects complete before continuing. Both operands of the comma operator are always evaluated.

Note that the comma operator in a function call does not guarantee an order of evaluation.

- Function-call operator. All arguments to a function are evaluated and all side effects complete before entry to the function. No order of evaluation among the arguments is specified.

- First operand of the conditional operator. The first operand of the conditional operator is completely evaluated and all side effects complete before continuing.

- The end of a full initialization expression (that is, an expression that is not part of another expression such as the end of an initialization in a declaration statement).

- The expression in an expression statement. Expression statements consist of an optional expression followed by a semicolon (;). The expression is evaluated for its side effects and there is a sequence point following this evaluation.

- The controlling expression in a selection (**if** or **switch**) statement. The expression is completely evaluated and all side effects complete before the code dependent on the selection is executed.

- The controlling expression of a **while** or **do** statement. The expression is completely evaluated and all side effects complete before any statements in the next iteration of the **while** or **do** loop are executed.

- Each of the three expressions of a **for** statement. The expressions are completely evaluated and all side effects complete before any statements in the next iteration of the **for** loop are executed.

- The expression in a **return** statement. The expression is completely evaluated and all side effects complete before control returns to the calling function.

Q18. What will be the output of below C code?

```c
#include <stdio.h>

int main()

{

int arr[10];

int i = 0;

arr[i] = i++;

printf("%d %d %d\n", arr[0], arr[1], i);

return 0;

}
```

ANSWER: 0 0 1

This is what most of the compilers are giving but here behaviour of program is undefined i, e output will vary compiler to compiler.

The sub expression i++ causes a side effect as it modifies the value of variable i which leads to undefined behaviour since i is also referenced elsewhere in the same expression. There is no way of knowing whether the reference will happen before or after the side effect--in fact, neither obvious interpretation might hold.

Q19. What will be the output of below C code?

```c
#include <stdio.h>

int main()

{

int i = 7;

printf("%d\n", i++ * i++);
```

return 0;

}

ANSWER: 49 (On Dev C++ and codepad)

56 (On Ideone)

Clearly, behaviour is undefined. Output will vary compiler to compiler.

Q20. What will be the output of below C code?

#include <stdio.h>

int main()

{

int i = 3;

i = i++;

printf("%d", i);

return 0;

}

ANSWER: 3 or 4 depend on your compiler.

Q21. Can we use explicit parentheses to force the order of evaluation as we want, and control these side effects?

ANSWER: No, We can't in general. Actually Operator precedence and explicit parentheses impose only a partial ordering on the evaluation of an expression. In the expression: f () + g () * h ()

Although we know that the multiplication will happen before the addition, there is no telling which of the three functions will be called first. In other words, precedence only partially specifies order of evaluation, where partially emphatically does not cover evaluation of operands.

Parentheses tell the compiler which operands go with which operators; they do *not* force the compiler to evaluate everything within the parentheses first. Adding explicit parentheses to the above expression to make it f () + (g () * h ()) would make no difference in the order of the function calls. Similarly, adding explicit parentheses to the expression from Q18 to make it

(i++) * (i++)   // won't work

Accomplishes nothing (since ++ already has higher precedence than *); the expression remains undefined with or without them. When you need to ensure the order of sub expression evaluation, you may need to use explicit temporary variables and separate statements.

Q22. Which function will be called first in below C code snippet?

```
printf("%d %d", f1(), f2());
```

ANSWER: The order of evaluation of the arguments to a function call in C is undefined. It's up to the compiler you are using. Some may call f2 () before f1 ().

Note: - The comma used for separating arguments in a function doesn't act as a comma operator. The comma operator does guarantee left-to right evaluation, but the commas separating the arguments in a function call are not comma operators. Hence we can't say which function will be called first.

Q23. In C, expression j = i++ * i++ is undefined whereas j = i++ && i++ is valid? Why is it so?

ANSWER: The C, standard states that:

The value which is stored in an object (By "object" we mean either a simple variable, or a cell of an array, or the location pointed to by a pointer) can be modified only once (by evaluation of expression) between two sequence points. And in Q16, I have already mentioned about sequence points. In first expression variable i is getting modified twice between two sequence points so expression is undefined but second expression is perfectly valid because a sequence point is occurring at && and variable i is getting modified once before and once after this sequence point. Refer to Q16. && (logical AND) creates a sequence point.

Q24. In C, expressions like a[i] = i++, i = i++ are undefined then why expression i = i + 1 is defined? Give Reason.

ANSWER: According to C standard if an object is to be modified within an expression then all accesses to that object within same expression must be for computing the value stored in that object. Hence expression a[i] = i++ is undefined as one of accesses of i (which belongs to a[i]) doesn't depend on the value that ends up being stored in i of RHS. In such case the compiler may not know whether the access should take place before or after the incremented value is stored. But in case of i = i + 1, it is perfectly valid because i accessed to determine the final value of i.

Q25. What will be the output of below C code?

#include <stdio.h>

int main()

{

int a = 3, b, c;

b = --a;

c = a--;

printf("%d %d %d\n", a, b, c);

return 0;

}

ANSWER: 1 2 2

Here we have prefix and postfix operators in our problem. The prefix increment operator adds one to its operand. This incremented value is used in the expression to get the result of the expression. The prefix decrement operator is similar to the prefix increment operator, except that the operand is decremented by one and the decremented result is used in the expression to get the value of the expression.

In the postfix form, the increment or decrement takes place after the value is used in expression evaluation.

In prefix increment or decrement operation the increment or decrement takes place before the value is used in expression evaluation.

Also precedence denotes the priority of operators. In other words if number of operators occur in an expression the priority in which the operators gets executes is decided by precedence of operators.

Associativity is the order in which an operator gets executes. Prefix and postfix gets the highest precedence among the operators and the associativity of these is from right to left. The operator gets executed from right to left in an expression.

Q26. What will be the output of below C code?

```c
#include <stdio.h>

int main()
{
int a = 5, b, c;

b = ++a + 5;

c = a++ + 5;

printf ("%d %d\n", b, c);

return 0;

}
```

ANSWER: 11 11

Output is obvious.

Q27. What will be the output of below C code?

#include <stdio.h>

int main()

{

int i = 0;

int v = i ? 3 : '2';

printf ("%d\n", v);

return 0;

}

ANSWER: 50

Note: - A ternary operator has the following form: exp1 ? exp2 : exp3. The expression exp1 is always evaluated first. Execution of exp2 and exp3 depends on the outcome exp1. If exp1 evaluates to 1 (true) then exp2 will be executed otherwise exp3 will be executed. Ternary operator has a return type that depends on exp2 and convertibility of exp3 into exp2 as per usual or overloaded conversion rules. If they are not convertible then compiler reports an error. So, make sure both the expressions exp2 and exp3 must have same return type or at least safely convertible types.

Output should be clear now and focus on exp3 of given question whose ASCII value is 50.

Q28. What will be the output of below C code?

#include <stdio.h>

int main()

{

int x, y, z;

x = y = z = 3;

printf ("x = %d y = %d z = %d\n", ++x, y++, ++z);

return 0;

}

ANSWER: 4 3 4

Here whether we go from left to right or right to left we will get same output. Also arguments are different.

Q29. What is lvalue and rvalue in C?

ANSWER: Expressions that refer to memory locations are called "l-value" expressions. An l-value represents a storage region's "locator" value, or a "left" value, implying that it can appear on the left of the equal sign (=). L-values are often identifiers.

The term "r-value" is sometimes used to describe the value of an expression and to distinguish it from an l-value. All l-values are r-values but not all r-values are l-values.

More important facts regarding lvalue and rvalue in C are given below:

Expressions referring to modifiable locations are called "modifiable l-values." A modifiable l-value cannot have an array type, an incomplete type, or a type with the **const** attribute. For structures and unions to be modifiable l-values, they must not have any members with the **const** attribute. The name of the identifier denotes a storage location, while the value of the variable is the value stored at that location.

An identifier is a modifiable l-value if it refers to a memory location and if its type is arithmetic, structure, union, or pointer. For example, if ptr is a pointer to a storage region, then *ptr is a modifiable l-value that designates the storage region to which ptr points.

Any of the following C expressions can be l-value expressions:

- An identifier of integral, floating, pointer, structure, or union type

- A subscript ([ ]) expression that does not evaluate to an array

- A member-selection expression (−> or.)

- A unary-indirection (*) expression that does not refer to an array

- An l-value expression in parentheses

- A **const** object (a non modifiable l-value)

Q30. What will be the output of below C code?

#include <stdio.h>

int main()

{

int i = 5;

printf ("%d", (++i)++);

return 0;

}

ANSWER: Compile time error.

In C, postfix and prefix increment or decrement operator require an lvalue expression as an operand and returns an rvalue. Hence, providing an rvalue or const qualified variables results into compilation error.

Q31. Will the below C code compile successfully?

#include <stdio.h>

int main()

{

```
int x = 10, y = 20;

(x, y) = 30;

printf ("y = %d", y);

return 0;

}
```

ANSWER: Compile time error.

In C, using the result of comma operator as an lvalue is not valid. In our given question we have (x, y) = 30 and here comma operator yields y as an lvalue which is used for storing an rvalue 30 which is not allowed in C.

Q32. What will be the output of below C code?

```
#include <stdio.h>

int main()

{

int a = 0, b = 1, c = 0;

char x = 'A', y = 'X';

if (a, y, x, b, c)

printf ("C\n");

else

printf ("C++");

return 0;

}
```

ANSWER: C++

Think of comma operator concept.

Q33. What will be the output of below code?

```c
#include <stdio.h>
int main()

{
int i = 3;

printf ("%d", i+++i);

return 0;

}
```

ANSWER: 7 (Ideone)

6 (codepad)

Clearly behaviour is undefined. Output will depend on compiler.

Q34. What will be the output of below C code?

```c
#include <stdio.h>

int main()

{
signed char ch = 0;

for (; ch >= 0; ch++);

printf ("%d\n", ch);

return 0;

}
```

ANSWER: -128

There is a semi colon after for () loop. The loop will continue until it doesn't get false. Since, i is a signed character, it can take value from -128 to 127. So in for () loop, i will keep incrementing and the condition is met till roll over happens. At the roll over, i will become -128 after 127, in that case condition is not met and control comes out of the for loop.

Q35. What will be the output of below C code?

```
#include <stdio.h>
int main()
{
int x = 0;
while (+(+x--) != 0)
x -= x++;
printf ("%d", x);
return 0;
}
```

ANSWER: -1

Here we have many operators like unary + operator, postfix ++ operator.

Unary + operator don't do anything. So the simplified condition becomes (i--)! = 0. So i will be compared with 0 and then decremented no matter whether condition is true or false. Since i is initialized to 0, the condition of while will be false at the first iteration itself but i will be decremented to -1. The body of while () loop never get executed. Hence, printf prints -1.

Q36. What will be the output of below C code?

```
#include <stdio.h>
int main()
{
```

```c
int i = 5;

printf ("%d", i = ++i == 6);

return 0;

}
```

ANSWER: 1

Prefix increment operator (++) has higher precedence than == and = operator in C. Hence, variable **i** will be incremented to 6 and then compared against 6 which is true and finally assignment operator (=) will assign 1 to **i**.

Q37. What will be the output of below C code?

```c
#include <stdio.h>

int main()

{

int a = 10, b = 20, c = 30;

if (c > b > a)

{

printf ("TRUE");

}

else

{

printf ("FALSE");

}

 return 0;

}
```

ANSWER: FALSE

Let us consider the condition inside if statement. Since there are two greater than (>) operators in expression "c > b > a", associativity of > is considered. Associativity of > is left to right. So, expression "c > b > a" is evaluated as ((c > b) > a) which is false.

Q38. What will be the output of below C code?

```
#include <stdio.h>

int main()

{

int a = 10, c;

c = (a > 30) ? return (20) : return (0);

printf ("%d", c);

return 0;

}
```

ANSWER: Well, most of you say- 0 but here code won't compile. Syntax says that **return** can't be used like above with ternary operator. Instead you can do like this:

return (a > 30 ? 20 : 0);

Q39. What will be the output of below C code?

```
#include <stdio.h>

int main()

{

printf ("%d", (printf("Let's learn"), printf("C")));

return 0;
```

}

ANSWER: Let's learn C 1

printf returns number of characters it has successfully printed. First printf prints "Let's learn" and return 11 whereas second printf returns 1 as it has printed only one character "C". Now, we have comma operator and comma operator evaluates it operands from left to right and returns the value returned by the rightmost expression. Thus, 1 will be printed finally by outermost printf on console.

Chapter-5

Functions In C

Q1. What is the importance of function prototype in C?

ANSWER: A function has three important features namely function name, the parameters (type, number and order) it accepts and its return type. Function prototype tells compiler about number of parameters function takes data-types of parameters and return type of function. By using this information, compiler cross checks function parameters and their data-type with function definition and function call. If we ignore function prototype, program may compile with warning, and may work properly. But sometimes, it will give strange output and it is very hard to find such programming mistakes/bugs.

Q2. What is the evaluation order of function parameters in C?

ANSWER: It totally depends on C compiler you are using.

Consider a pseudo code in C given below:

void func (int x, int y);   // function prototype

int i = 3;

func (i++, i++);   // function call

There is no guarantee that the increments will be evaluated in any particular order. Either increment might happen first. **func** () might get the arguments 3, 4 or it might get 4, 3 or even 3, 3.

Q3. How parameters are passed in a function in C?

ANSWER: In C, function parameters are always passed by value.

Q4. What are the return types of a function in C?

ANSWER: In C, functions can return any data type except array and function. We can get around this limitation by returning a pointer to an array or a pointer to a function.

Q5. Can we return multiple values from a function in C?

ANSWER: A function in C can return only one value. But we can make the function to return multiple values. If a function can return a pointer then this is possible. We can declare the function such that, it returns a structure type user defined variable or pointer to it. Since, structures in C can hold multiple values of different data types. If we want the function to return multiple values of same data types, we could return the pointer to array of that data types. We can also make the function return multiple values by passing the address of arguments i, e by passing pointer to those arguments.

Q6. What is the meaning of using **static** before function declaration?

ANSWER: Consider a function below which has static qualifier with it-

static int func (int x, int y, int z)

{

return (x * y * z);

}

ANSWER: In C, functions are global by default. Unlike global functions, access to static functions is restricted to the file where they are declared. We can have file level encapsulation using static variables/functions in C because when we make a global variable static, access to the variable becomes limited to the file in which it is declared.

Q7. What is the meaning of using **extern** before function declaration?

ANSWER: It does not matter anything. A function having **extern** qualifier or without it, works in same way. **extern** keyword is used for global variables. Functions are global anyways in C, so adding extern doesn't add anything.

Q8. What will be the output of below C code?

```c
#include <stdio.h>

void func(int ,int);                    //function prototype

int main()

{

int x = 4, y = 2;

func(4, 2);                             //function call (call by value)

printf("x = %d y = %d\n", x, y);

return 0;

}

void func(int x, int y)

{

x = x * x;

y = y * y;

}
```

ANSWER: x = 4 y = 2

Shocked!!! But this is what we will get because here arguments have been passed by their values i, e call by value. The variables x and y in main () and func () have different scopes. They are located in different memory location. Inside func () we have calculated the product of x and y and stored in x and y itself but as soon as control passes out of func (), these x and y are no more in memory and control comes to main () block where x and y of this scope remains alive and hence we get the required output.

Q9. What will be the output of below C code?

```c
#include <stdio.h>

void func(int *, int *);

int main()
{
int x = 4, y = 2;
func(&x, &y);                     //call by reference
printf("x = %d y = %d\n", x, y);
return 0;
}
void func(int *x, int *y)
{
*x = *x * *x;
*y = *y * *y;
}
```

ANSWER: x = 16 y = 4

Here while calling func(&x, &y) we are passing the address of variables. Inside **func** () we have received the addresses of the variables and then doing arithmetic operations on these variables. Since we are doing operation at memory level i, e we have directly accessed their memory location and storing the final values in their memory location. This effect is permanently because it is "call by reference" in C.

Q10. What will be the output of below C code?

```c
#include <stdio.h>
```

```
int x = 0;

int func1()

{

return x;

}

int func2()

{

int x = 2;

return func1();

}

int main()

{

printf("%d", func2());

return 0;

}
```

ANSWER: 0

In C, variables are always statically (or lexically) scoped. Binding of **x** inside **func1** () to global variable **x** is defined at compile time and not dependent on who is calling it. Hence, output for the above program will be 0.

Q11. What will be the output of below C code?

```
#include <stdio.h>

int func1(int);

int func2(int);
```

```c
int main()
{
int a, b, c = 2;
c *= 3;
a = func1(c);
b = func2(c);
printf ("%d %d %d\n", c, b, a);
return 0;
}
int t = 8;
int func1(int x)
{
x += -5;
t -= 4;
return (x + t);
}
int func2(int x)
{
x = 1;
t += x;
return (x + t);
}
```

Q12. What will be the output of below C code?

```c
#include <stdio.h>
int func(int);
int main()
{
int x, y;
for (x = 1; x<=4; x++)
{
y = func(x);
printf ("y = %d", y);
}
int func(int x)
{
static int a = 1;
int b = 3;
a += x;
return (a + x + b);
}
```

ANSWER: 6 9 13 18

Inside func () we have declared a static variable **a**, and as we know that value of a **static** variable persists between several function calls whereas variable **b** has **auto** storage class. Whenever the control comes under func (), **b** will re-initialized to 3 but **a** will not, its old value will be available for current operation. Rest of the things are clear and obvious.

Q13. What will be the output of below C code?

```
#include <stdio.h>

int func();

int main()

{

for (func(); func(); func())

printf ("%d ", func());

return 0;

}

int func()

{

static int x = 16;

return (x--);

}
```

ANSWER: 14 11 8 5 2

As we have a **static** variable **x** inside func (), so its value will preserved for further function calls. Also, we have postfix decrement operator so first old value of **x** will be returned and then decremented.

Q14. What will be the output of below C code?

```
#include <stdio.h>

int func(static int x, static int y, static int z)
```

```
{
return (x + y + z);

}
int main()

{
int x, y, z;

x = y = z = 3;

printf ("%d ", func(x, y, z));

return 0;

}
```

ANSWER: Compile time error.

In C, function parameters can never be **static** because the static keyword means that a variable may have only and exactly one instance in its scope, and that instance is invisible out of its scope. Neither of these requirements makes sense for a function argument: it may be called multiple times, at a different memory address, and as it's meant for communication, it has to be visible to the outer world.

Note- We may have a static function, a **global static** variable and a **local static** variable in C but function parameters can never be **static.**

Q15. What will be the output of below C code?

```
#include <stdio.h>

int func1(int);

int func2(int);

int main()
```

```c
{
int x = 35, y;

y = func1(x);

printf ("y = %d ", y);

return 0;

}
int func1(int m)

{
m++;

return (m = func2 (++m));

}
int func2(int m)

{
m++;

return (m);

}
```

ANSWER: y = 38

Q16. What error will compiler give on compiling the below C function?

```c
int func(int x, int y)

{
int x;

x = 2;
```

return (x * 4);

}

ANSWER: Re-declaration of x

Note- Re-declaration of a function is not an error whereas re-definition is an error.

Q17. What will be the output of below C code?

#include <stdio.h>

void

func();

int main()

{

int x = 20;

x = func ();

printf ("%d\n", x);

return 0;

}

void func()

{

printf ("Concepts In C");

}

ANSWER: Compile time error.

Here we have declared func () as returning void, still we are trying to collect the value returned by func () in variable x. This leads to compilation error.

Q18. What will be the output of below C code?

```c
#include <stdio.h>
int a, b;
void func();
int main ()
{
static int a = 1;    /* line 1 */
func();
a += 1;
func();
printf ("%d %d\n", a, b) ;
}
void func()
{
static int a = 2;    /* line 2 */
int b = 1;
a += ++b;
printf ("%d %d\n", a, b);
}
```

ANSWER: 4 2

6 2

2 0

Here, we have global variables **a** and **b** and also inside func (), local variables **a** and **b.** In C, local variables hide global variables. When func () is called first time, the local variable **b** becomes 2 and local variable **a** becomes 4. When func () is called second time, same instance of local **a** is used but a new instance of local **b** is created because **a** is static and **b** is auto. Rest of the things are simple to get the outputs.

Q19. What will be the output of above question if Line 1 is replaced by auto int a = 1, Line 2 is replaced by register int a = 2?

ANSWER: 4 2

       4 2

       2 0

Try this at your own.

Q20. What will be the output of below C code?

```c
#include <stdio.h>

int func(int);

int main()
{
int x = 12;
x = func(x = func(x = func(x)));
printf ("%d", x);
return 0;
}
int func(int x)
{
```

```
return (++x);

}
```

ANSWER: 15

This one is a simple program. Here, innermost **func** () will be called first with argument **x** = **12**. Value returned by **func** () is 13 and hence new argument for second **func** () call will be 13 and this time **func** () will return 14 and now 14 is the argument for outermost **func** () call and hence **func** () will return 15 which is our required output.

Q21. What will be the output of below C code?

```
#include <stdio.h>

int func();

int x;

int main()

{

while (1)

{

if (!x)

{

func();

break;

}

else

main();

}
```

```
printf ("C++");

return 0;

}

int func()

{

printf ("C");

return 0;

}
```

ANSWER: C C++

Here, variable **x** has global scope and will contain 0 as its initial value. So, **if** () block becomes true and **func** () is called which prints C and then in **main** () C++ gets printed.

Q22. What will be the output of below C code?

```
#include <stdio.h>

int func();

int main()

{

int a = 10, b;

while (a > 0)

{

b = func(a);

--a;

}
```

```c
printf ("%d", b);

return 0;

}

int func(int m)

{

static int x = 0;

x += m;

return (x);

}
```

ANSWER: 55

Inside func () we have a **static** variable **x** which is being added to variable **m** for 10 times. If you'll observe carefully then you will see, program is actually calculating the sum of first 10 natural numbers.

Q23. What will be the output of below C code?

```c
#include <stdio.h>

int func(int, int);

int main()

{

int i = 135, a = 135, k;

k = func (!++i, !a++);

printf ("i = %d a = %d k = %d\n", i, a, k);

return 0;

}
```

```
int func(int x, int y)

{

int c;

c = x + y;

return c;

}
```

ANSWER: i = 136 a = 136 k = 0

Observe the function call in main (). Inside func () we have pre-increment, post-increment and local NOT operator. In first argument, ++ precedes variable i, its value is increased to 136 and then ! operator negates it to give 0. This 0 is however not stored in variable i but is passed to func () whereas in second argument we have post-increment so first ! operator will negate a then func () will be called with 0 argument and then variable a will b increased to 136 in its scope. So, here func (0, 0) will be called. Rest of the things are clear.

Q24. Recursion is usually slow than loops, why is it so? Explain.

ANSWER: Yes, recursion is slower than our iterative loops. It is because Recursive procedures are slightly slower than iterative ones, because of the overhead of procedure calls and recursive function uses a lot of stack space.

Q25. What will be the output of below C code?

```
#include <stdio.h>

int func(int n)

{

if (n == 4)    // base case

return n;
```

else

return 2 * func(n+1);

}

int main()

{

printf ("%d", func(2));

return 0;

}

ANSWER: 16

Here we are dealing with recursion. func () is called recursively until base case does not become true. Initially func () is called with 2 and get stored in **n** but **n** is not equal to 4 hence else block gets executed and now func () is called 3 (2 + 1). Again if () block becomes false and func () is called with argument 4 (3 + 1) and this time if () block is true and hence base case value is returned i, e 4. Now func () will not be called anymore and control comes back to the scope of func (3) where n = 3 and hence control will start executing the next instruction from where it had left when a recursive call was made. Now, func (3) return back 8 to func (2) and control comes back to func (2) scope where n = 2 and value which will be returned back to main () is 16, which is our required output.

Q26. What will be the output of below C code?

#include <stdio.h>

void func(int);

int main()

{

int x = 3;

```
func (x);

return 0;

}

void func(int x)

{

if (x > 0)

{

func (--x);

printf ("%d ", x);

func (--x);

}

}
```

ANSWER: 0 1 2 0

Q27. What will be the output of below C code?

```
#include <stdio.h>

int func(int, int);

int main()

{

int m = 4, n = 3;

func (m, n);

return 0;

}
```

```c
int func(int m, int n)

{

if (m == 0)

return n;

else

return func (m - 1, m + n);

}
```

ANSWER: 13

Q28. What will be the output of below C code?

```c
#include <stdio.h>

int func(int n)

{

if (n <= 1)    // base case

return 1;

if (n%2 == 0)

return func(n/2);

return func(n/2) + func(n/2 + 1);

}

int main()

{

printf ("%d", func(11));

return 0;
```

```
}
```

ANSWER: 5

Q29. What will be the output of below C code?

```
#include <stdio.h>

int main()

{

printf ("Concepts In C");

main();   // recursive call

}
```

ANSWER: The program will keep printing "Concepts In C" till stack does not overflow. Recursive functions uses stack that is why too many recursive function calls lead to stack overflow which is a run-time error.

Q30. What will be the output of below C code?

```
#include <stdio.h>

int main()

{

int x = 1;

if (!x)

printf ("Recursion is slow than iterative loops\n");

else

{

x = 0;

printf ("Recursion many times score over loops\n");
```

```
main();   // recursive call
}
return 0;
}
```

ANSWER: Recursion many times score over loops

Recursion many times score over loops

....

....

It goes into infinite loop and will keep printing till stack doesn't overflow.

Note: Try changing the variable **x** inside main () from **auto** to **static**. Then observe the output.

Q31. What will be the output of below C code?

```
#include <stdio.h>
int g(int);
int main()
{
int n = 1;
printf ("%d", g(n));
return 0;
}
int g(int n)
{
  static int i = 1;
```

if (n >= 5)

return n;

n += i;

++i;

return g(n);

}

ANSWER: 7

Since variable **i** is of static type hence it will be initialized only once. Also n is not equal to 5 so before calling a recursive call of g (), we are increasing **n** and **i** then g () is called recursively. Here firstly g (1), g (2), g (4) and g (7) will be called recursively. When g (7) will be called, **n** will be more than 5 hence base case value will be returned back to main () which is printed by printf in side main ().

Q32. What will be the output of below C code?

#include <stdio.h>

int g(int n);

int main()

{

int n = 5;

printf ("%d", g(n));

return 0;

}

int g(int n)

{

static int r = 0;

if (n <= 0)

return 1;

if (n > 3)

{

r = n;

return (g(n − 2) + 2);

}

else

return (g(n − 1) + r);

}

ANSWER: 18

Here trace the function calls as:

g (0) + 5 = 6 ⟶ g (1) + 5 = 11 ⟶ g (2) + 5 = 16 ⟶ g (3) + 2 = 18.

which is our output.

Q33. What will the following function do in a C program?

```c
#include <stdio.h>

void func()

{

int m = 0, n = 1;

int i;

for (i = 0; i < 15; i++)
```

```
{

printf ("%d ", m);

m = m + n;

n = m - n;

}

return 0;

}
```

ANSWER: The function func () will print first 15 fibonacci numbers.

Q34. Is it necessary to mention prototype of a function even if one have already defined the function before calling it?

ANSWER: No, it is not mandatory. Rule says that if a function has not been defined before its actual call then one must mention its prototype otherwise it will lead to compilation error.

Q35. What will be the output of below C code?

```
#include <stdio.h>

int func (int x)

{

return (++x);

}

int main()

{

int i;

for (i = 1; i <= 10; func(i))
```

printf ("Hello");

return 0;

}

ANSWER: Hello will be printed infinite times.

Inside for () loop where increment is done, there we are calling func () and variable **i** is passed by value not by its reference as func () argument. Inside func () variable **x** is holding the copy of variable **i** and this **i** (inside func) and **i** of main () is different. Though we are incrementing **i** but inside func () scope and this effect is not visible inside main (). Hence loop never terminates and goes into infinite loop.

Q36. What will be the output of below C code?

```
#include <stdio.h>

int main()
{
void func1(int);
void func2(int);
void func3(int);
int n = 2;
func1(n);
func2(n);
return 0;
}
void func1(int x)
{
```

```c
++x;

func3(x);

}
void func2(int y)

{

--y;

func3(y);

}
void func3(int z)

{

printf ("%d", z);

}
```

ANSWER: Compilation error.

Here we have placed func3 () inside main () so scope has been changed from global to local (functions in C have global scope by default). Hence when func3 () is called from func2 () and func1 (), compiler thinks that neither prototype nor function definition has been done. This results into compilation error.

Note- Try placing func3 () above main (), you will get 3 1 as output.

Chapter-6

Macros & Preprocessors

Q1. What is C preprocessor? Mention some of its benefits.

ANSWER: The C preprocessor is a macro processor that is used automatically by the C compiler to transform your program before actual compilation. It is called a macro processor because it allows you to define macros, which are brief abbreviations for longer constructs.

The C preprocessor provides four separate facilities that you can use as you see fit:

- Inclusion of header files. These are files of declarations that can be substituted into your program.

- Macro expansion. You can define macros, which are abbreviations for arbitrary fragments of C code, and then the C preprocessor will replace the macros with their definitions throughout the program.

- Conditional compilation. Using special preprocessing directives, you can include or exclude parts of the program according to various conditions.

- Line control. If you use a program to combine or rearrange source files into an intermediate file which is then compiled, you can use line control to inform the compiler of where each source line originally came from.

Q2. What will be the output of below C code?

#include <stdio.h>

#define SQR(x) x*x

int main()

```
{

int x;

x = 49/SQR(7);

printf ("%d", x);

return 0;

}
```

ANSWER: 49

Before compilation, preprocessor replaces the SQR(7) by 7 * 7 and hence x =
49 / 7 * 7, which evaluates to 49.

___

Q3.What will be the output of below C code?

```
#include <stdio.h>

#define SQR(x) ((x)*(x))

int main()

{

int x;

x = 49/SQR(7);

printf ("%d", x);

return 0;

}
```

ANSWER: 1

Before compilation, preprocessor replaces the SQR(7) by (7*7) and hence x
= 49/ (7*7), which evaluates to 1.

___

Q4. What will be the output of below C code?

```c
#include <stdio.h>

#define VAL 10

int main()

{

printf ("%d", VAL);

#define VAL 50

printf ("%d", VAL);

return 0;

}
```

ANSWER: 10 50

We can redefine a preprocessor directive in C. Some compiler may give a warning. Preprocessor will always take the most recent value of 'macro template' VAL and replaces it with 'macro expansion' i, e 10 and 50 in this case.

Q5. What will be the output of below C code?

```c
#include <stdio.h>

#define CUBE(x) (x*x*x)

int main()

{

printf ("%d", CUBE(1+2));

return 0;

}
```

ANSWER: 7

Preprocessor will replace the macro template CUBE(1+2) by 1+2*1+2*1+2 this evaluates to 7.

Q6. What is the extension of the intermediate file which is created by preprocessing the source code in C?

ANSWER: .i

In C, preprocessor is a type of program which pre-processes the source code and generates an intermediate file with **.i** extension which is passed to the compiler for compilation.

Q7. What will be the output of below C code?

```
# include <stdio.h>
# define scanf "%s Concepts In C"
int main()
{
 printf (scanf, scanf);
 return 0;
}
```

ANSWER: %s Concepts In C Concepts In C

Preprocessor will replace the two macro templates with "%s Concepts In C" and hence printf ("%s Concepts In C", "%s Concepts In C") will be executed.

Q8. What will be the output of below C code?

```
#include <stdio.h>
#define PRODUCT(x, y)  x*y
int main()
```

```
{
int m = 5, n = 7;

printf ("%d", PRODUCT(m+3, n-2));

return 0;

}
```

ANSWER: 24

Preprocessor will replace PRODUCT (m+3, n-2) by 5 + 3 * 7 – 2 which is equal to 24.

Q9. What will be the output of below C code?

```
#include <stdio.h>

#define  X 3

#if  X == 3

#define  Y 3

#else

#define Y 5

#endif

 int main()

{

 printf("%d", Y);

return 0;

}
```

ANSWER: 3

In C, **#if** is a directive which can be used to test whether, an expression evaluates to true or false. If the result is true, then subsequent lines upto

#else, #elif, or **#endif** are compiled, otherwise they are skipped.

Q10. What will be output of above question if macro X is undefined?

#include <stdio.h>

#define X

#if X == 3

#define Y 3

#else

#define Y 5

#endif

int main()

{

printf("%d", Y);

return 0;

}

ANSWER: 5

In C, if a macro is not defined, the pre-processor assigns 0 to it by default. Hence, the control goes to the conditional else part and 5 is printed. Hence macro template X has 0 as its macro template which is false (0).

Q11. What will be the output of below C code?

#include <stdio.h>

#define ISUPPER(x) (x >= 65 && x <= 90)

#define ISLOWER(x) (x >= 97 && x<= 122)

#define ISALPHA(x) (ISUPPER(x) || ISLOWER(x))

int main()

{

char ch = 'A';

if (ISALPHA(ch))

printf ("ch contains an alphabet");

else

printf ("ch doesn't contain an alphabet");

return 0;

}

ANSWER: ch contains an alphabet

The first and second macro has the criteria for checking whether their argument X is an upper or lower case alphabet. These two criteria have been combined in third macro. ISALPHA when executed, if statement has been changed to if (ch >= 65 && ch <= 90 || ch >= 97 && ch <= 122). Rest of the things are simple to get the output.

Q12. Do macros have local scope?

ANSWER: No. During preprocessing wherever a macro template is found, the preprocessor will replace that template by its macro expansion.

Q13. What will be the output of below C code?

#include <stdio.h>

#define X

#if !X

```
printf ("C");

#else

printf ("C++");

#endif

int main()

{

  return 0;

}
```

ANSWER: C

Here default value of macro X is 0 because macro X is undefined. Rest of the things are clear and simple to guess the output.

Q14. What is token pasting operator in C?

ANSWER: The double-number-sign or "token-pasting" operator (##), which is sometimes called the "merging" operator, is used in both object-like and function-like macros. It permits separate tokens to be joined into a single token and therefore cannot be the first or last token in the macro definition.

Q15. What will be the output of below C code?

```
#include <stdio.h>

#define FUNC(x, y)  x##y

int main()

{

int var2 = 30;

int var21 = 40;

printf("%d", FUNC(var2, 1));
```

return 0;

}

ANSWER: 40

Token pasting operator will merge two tokens namely var2 and 1 as a single token which is var21 and this is of int type having value 40.

Q16. What will be the output of below C code?

```
#include <stdio.h>

#define FUN(n, a, i, m)  m##a##i##n

#define MAIN macro(n, a, i, m)

 int MAIN()

{

 printf("Concepts In C");

 return 0;

}
```

ANSWER: Concepts In C

Try to think this one at your own. Think of token pasting operator.

Q17. What will be the output of below C code?

```
#include <stdio.h>

#define CMP(X, Y)  X == Y

int main()

{

 #if CMP(X, 0)

 printf("C");
```

#else

printf("C++");

#endif

return 0;

}

ANSWER: C

The conditional macro #if CMP(X, 0) is expanded to #if X == 0. After the pre-processing is over, all the undefined macros are initialized with default value 0. Since macro X has not been defined, it is initialized with 0. So, C is printed.

Q18. What do the headers files in C contain?

ANSWER: Headers files contain many preprocessor directives, structure, union and enum declaration, typedef declarations, global variable declarations and external function declarations.

Q19. What will be the output of below C code?

#include <stdio.h>

int main()

{

#ifdef NOTE

int a;

a = 10;

#else

int a;

a = 20;

```
#endif

printf("%d", a);

return 0;

}
```

ANSWER: 20

Macro NOTE is undefined so default value of NOTE will be 0 and hence #else block gets executed and printf prints 20.

Q20. What is difference between #include <stdio.h> and #include "stdio.h"?

ANSWER: <stdio.h> is a header file which available in include directory of the system. When we write #include<stdio.h> preprocessor search for it in predefined include directory only and not out of this directory. But when we write "stdio.h" processor starts searching not only in predefined include directory but also in current working directory as well.

Q21. What will be the output of below C code?

```
#include <stdio.h>
#define PRINT(int)  printf("%d", int)

int main()

{

int a = 4, b = 5, c = 6;

PRINT(a);

PRINT(b);

PRINT(c);

return 0;

}
```

Q22. What is Stringizing Operator (#) in C?

ANSWER: The number-sign or stringizing operator (#) converts macro parameters to string literals without expanding the parameter definition. It is used only with macros that take arguments. If it precedes a formal parameter in the macro definition, the actual argument passed by the macro invocation is enclosed in quotation marks and treated as a string literal. The string literal then replaces each occurrence of a combination of the stringizing operator and formal parameter within the macro definition.

Q23. What will be the output of below C code?

#include <stdio.h>

#define PRINT(int) printf(#int " " = %d ", int)

int main()

{

int a = 4, b = 5, c = 6;

PRINT(a);

PRINT(b);

PRINT(c);

return 0;

}

ANSWER: a = 4 b = 5 c = 6

Think of stringizing operator (#) work. Here after macro expansion, printf will look like printf ("a" " " = %d", a). After this two quotes get concatenated and finally printf becomes printf ("a = %d", a).

Q24. What will be the output of below C code?

```c
#include <stdio.h>

#define FUNC(arr)  (sizeof (arr) / sizeof (arr[0]))

int main()

{

int d;

int arr[] = {11, 22, 33, 44, 55};

for (d = -1; d < FUNC(arr) - 1; d++)

printf("%d ", arr[d + 1]);

return 0;

}
```

ANSWER: Nothing will be printed on console.

Here we have taken an array of length 5. Whenever **sizeof** operator is used with name of an array, then **sizeof** returns total memory occupied by that array whereas sizeof (arr [0]) will return 2 or 4 bytes for integer type. Hence expression - sizeof (arr) / sizeof (arr [0]) will return total number of elements in the given array. FUNC is a macro and after preprocessing, FUNC (arr) – 1 will be replaced by 5 (no of elements in our array arr) which is an unsigned number because return type of **sizeof** is always unsigned integer which is being compared against a signed integer **d**. In this comparison -1 is promoted to unsigned integer. -1 in unsigned format is represented as all its bit are set to 1 (i.e. 0xffffffff), which is too big number and after substituting value of macro, for loop look like this- for (d = -1; 0xffffffff < 5; d++).

In above loop indeed 0xffffffff is not less than 5, that's why for loop condition fails and program exits from loop without printing anything.

Q25. What will be the output of below C code?

```c
#include <stdio.h>
```

```
#define PR(a)  printf("%d ", a);

#define PRINT(a, b, c)  PR(a);PR(b);PR(c);

#define MAX(a, b)  (a<b ? b : a)

int main()

{

int x = 1,y = 2;

PRINT(MAX(x++,y), x, y);

PRINT(MAX(x++,y), x, y);

return 0;

}
```

ANSWER: 2 2 2 3 4 2

Q26. What is the benefit of using #define to declare a constant?

ANSWER: There are several benefits of using #define to declare a constant. Use of #define technique enables you to declare a constant in one place and use it throughout your program. This helps make your programs more maintainable, because you need to maintain only the #define statement and not several instances of individual constants throughout your program. Besides being the most common method of declaring constants, it also takes up the least memory. Constants defined in this manner are simply placed directly into your source code, with no variable space allocated in memory. Also Constants defined with the #define method can also be overridden using the #undef preprocessor directive.

Q27. Use of **const** is a better alternative than #define in some cases. Why is it so? Explain.

ANSWER: It is so because while using **const** programmers can control its scope of operation. **const** can have a local scope (when placed inside a function) or can have global scope (when placed outside a function). By using #define, effect is throughout the program whereas using **const**, one can simply control the scope issue.

Q28. What is the benefit of using an enum rather than #define constant?

ANSWER: The use of an enumeration constant (enum) has many advantages over using the traditional symbolic constant style of #define. These advantages include a lower maintenance requirement, improved program readability, and better debugging capability. The first advantage is that enumerated constants are generated automatically by the compiler. Conversely, symbolic constants must be manually assigned values by the programmer.

Q29. What will be the output of below C code?

#include <stdio.h>

#define TOTAL_NUM(arr) (sizeof (arr)/sizeof (arr[0]))

#define PRINT(expr) printf("%s : %d\n", #expr, (expr))

int main()

```
{
int arr[] = {0001, 0010, 0100, 1000};
int i;
for (i = 0; i < TOTAL_NUM(arr); i++)
PRINT(arr[i]);
return 0;
}
```

ANSWER: arr[i] : 1

arr[i] : 8

arr[i] : 64

arr[i] : 1000

Q30. What will be the output of below C code?

```c
#include <stdio.h>

#define PRINT(expr) printf ("%s: %d\n", #expr, (expr))

int max(int x, int y)
{
(x > y) ? return x : return y;
}

int main()
{
 int x = 10, y = 20;

PRINT(x);

PRINT(y);

PrintInt(max(x, y));

return 0;

}
```

ANSWER: Compilation error.

return can't be used with ternary operator as shown in this program. To make our program successfully compile replace the body of max () with this-

return (x > y ? x : y);

Chapter-7

Pointers & Arrays

Q1. What is a generic pointer in C?

ANSWER: When a variable is declared as being a pointer to type void it is known as a generic pointer. Since you cannot have a variable of type void, the pointer will not point to any data and therefore cannot be dereference. It is still a pointer though, to use it you just have to cast it to another kind of pointer first. Such type of pointer in C is known as generic pointer.

Q2. What is a dangling pointer in C?

ANSWER: A pointer that don't point to a valid object of the appropriate type. In other words, a pointer becomes a dangling pointer when the block of memory it points to, is no more available but the pointer still points to that freed memory location even though, the reference has been deleted or may be now used for other purposes.

Q3. What is a null pointer in C? Give examples.

ANSWER: A null pointer is a special pointer that is known not to point anywhere.

Examples: - 1. int *ptr = (char *)0;

    2. float *ptr = (float *)0;

    3. char *ptr = (char *)0;

    4. double *ptr = (double *)0;

    5. char *ptr = '\0';

    6. int *ptr = NULL;

Q4. What is NULL in C? How can you declare a null pointer constant in C?

ANSWER: NULL is macro in C having macro expansion value 0, defined in stdio.h; stddef.h headers files as #define NULL 0. The C library Macro NULL is the value of a null pointer constant. It may be defined as —

Macro: void * NULL. This is a null pointer constant. You can also use 0 or (void *) 0 as a null pointer constant, but using NULL is cleaner because it makes the purpose of the constant more evident.

Q5. What is address operator in C?

ANSWER: The unary address-of operator (**&**) takes the address of its operand and yields a pointer to its operand. The operand of the address-of operator can be either a function designator or an l-value that designates an object that is not a bit field and is not declared with the register storage-class specifier.

Q6. What is deference operator or indirection operator in C?

ANSWER: The dereference operator or indirection operator, denoted by "*" (i.e. an asterisk), is a unary operator that include pointer variables. It operates on a pointer variable, and returns an l-value equivalent to the value at the pointer address. This is called deference operator.

Q7. What will be the output of below C code?

```
#include <stdio.h>

int main()

{

int i , *ptr1;

char ch, *ptr2;

float f, *ptr3;

i = 64;

ch = 'B';

f = 1.414

ptr1 = &i;
```

```
ptr2 = &ch;

ptr3 = &f;

printf ("Address in ptr1 = %u ", ptr1);

printf ("Value stored in ptr1 = %d\n", *ptr1);

printf ("Address in ptr2 = %u ", ptr2);

printf ("Value stored in ptr2 = %c\n", *ptr2);

printf ("Address in ptr3 = %u ", ptr3);

printf ("Value stored in ptr3 = %f\n", *ptr3);

return 0;

}
```

ANSWER: Address in ptr1 = 3217502696 Value stored in ptr1 = 64

Address in ptr2 = 3217502695 Value stored in ptr2 = B

Address in ptr3 = 3217502700 Value stored in ptr3 = 1.414000

Here we have declared three variables and their respective pointers which hold the addresses of these three variables. printf prints the address of each variables using **%u** format specifier. The addresses have been assigned by the compiler and may vary for your system. Using deference operator, we have accessed the values stored in each variables. Here, when we have assigned values to each variables then binary equivalent of each value have been stored in each memory's location. Hence variable **i** contain binary equivalent of 64 i, e 0100000000000000 gets stored inside **i** (consider 16-bit compiler for convenience). In similar ways, variables **ch** contains binary equivalent of 'B' whose ASCII value is 66 and binary representation is 0100001000000000, variable **f** is of float type and it contains 0000000100000000, binary equivalent of 1.414. Also when we assign address of any variable to a pointer of its type then only the address of first byte of memory is stored inside the pointer. Hence, pointer ptr1 stores only the address of the first byte of the memory location where integer i is stored. Similarly, pointer ptr3 contain only first byte out of four bytes occupied by **float** variable f.

Q8. What will be the output of below C code?

```
#include <stdio.h>

int main()

{

int i = 532;

float f = 1.414

char *ptr1, *ptr2;

ptr1 = (char *) &i;

ptr2 = (char *) &f;

printf ("Address in ptr1 = %u ", ptr1);

printf ("Value stored in ptr1 = %d\n", *ptr1);

printf ("Address in ptr2 = %u ", ptr2);

printf ("Value stored in ptr2 = %d\n", *ptr2);

return 0;

}
```

ANSWER: Address in ptr1 = 3213637896 Value stored in ptr1 = 20

   Address in ptr2 = 3213637900 Value stored in ptr2 = -0.329215

Surprised..!! But this is what we will get on running this code on a **little endian** machine like INTEL. The addresses have been correctly printed by printf () but values stored has not been correctly printed. Why is it so? Well, through this question, my intention is to give some good concepts in pointers which are not given in many books which I have read during my initial learning stages. In this question, we have assigned the address of both integer variable **i** and float variable **f** in a pointer of **char** type by typecasting those addresses into a proper type. But second printf () didn't print 532 but it printed 20 because as I have already mentioned in previous question that whenever we assign a value to variable then actually binary equivalent of that value is stored inside that variable. Also pointer will hold only the first byte of memory location where the variable has been kept. Thus variable **i** will contain 0000001000010100 (binary equivalent of 532 on 16-bit compiler) but in **little endian** machines like INTEL, last byte of binary representation of the multi byte data-type is stored first i, e 00010100 will be stored first then to next memory location, 00000010 will be stored. 00010100 is nothing but 20 and ptr1 is of **char** type pointer and hence ptr1 will contain only first byte of the address where 00010100 is stored and will fetch decimal value of this binary number on dereferencing ptr1(*ptr1) and this is what gets printed by printf (). Same thing happens with float variable **f**. Do this at your own for better understanding.

Note: - Always store the address of an integer variable in an integer pointer, if you want to access an integer value stored in a variable using its address. Same thing applies for float data type as well. Actually, this applies for every data type in C.

Q9. What is little endian and big endian architecture?

ANSWER: Little and big endian are two ways of storing multi byte data-types (int, float, etc). In little endian machines, last byte of binary representation of the multi byte data-type is stored first. On the other hand, in big endian machines, first byte of binary representation of the multi byte data-type is stored first.

Let's consider an integer variable x = 4 and we are using 16-bit compiler like Borland Turbo C++ and binary equivalent of 4 is 0000000000000100 then in **little endian** machine, last 8-bits (00000100) will be stored first and then other 8-bits (00000000) to next memory location but **big endian** machines will do reverse of **little endian** machines.

Q10. What will be the output of below C code?

```
#include<stdio.h>

int main()

{

int x;

char *ch

ch = (char *) &x;

x = 512;

ch[0] = 1;

ch[1] = 2;

printf ("%d", x);

return 0;

}
```

ANSWER: The output of such a problem is machine dependent. Little endian machine will give 513 whereas big endian machine will give 258. Let's explore what is happening behind the scene. Binary equivalent of 512 is 00000010 00000000. But when compiler encounters ch[0] = 1 and ch[1] = 2 then our bit is changed to 00000001 00000010 which is representation of 513 in a little endian machine. But in a big endian machine, when we do ch[0] = 1 and ch[1] = 2, the number is changed to 00000001 00000010 which is representation of 258 in a big endian machine.

Q11. Write a C code to determine endianness of your machine?

ANSWER:

```c
#include <stdio.h>

int main()

{

unsigned int x = 1;

char *ch = (char*) &x;

if (*ch)

printf ("Little endian);

else

printf ("Big endian");

return 0;

}
```

We have declared a character pointer **ch** which is pointing to an unsigned integer **x**. proper typecasting must be done when we are assigning address of one data type to pointer of another data type. Size of a character in C is 1 byte and hence when pointer **ch** is de-referenced, then **ch** will contain only first byte of integer. If machine is **little endian** then *ch will yield 1 otherwise 0. Accordingly if () or else block gets executed.

Q12. What will be the output of below C code?

```c
#include <stdio.h>

int *func()    // function definition

{

int x = 10;

return (&x);

}
```

```
int main()

{

int *ptr;

ptr = func();

printf ("%d ", ptr);

printf ("%d", *ptr);

return 0;

}
```

ANSWER: GARBAGE value will be printed.

Here we have declared a function func () which takes no parameters but returns an integer pointer. Inside func (), an integer variable **x** has been defined which has auto storage class hence when func () returns the address **x** and control comes in main () block, variable being a local variable dies and no more available in the memory location which is pointed by **ptr**. So, inside main (), printf () will print some garbage values. To overcome this issue, we may use **static** keyword before variable **x**.

Q13. What will be the output of below C code?

```
#include <stdio.h>

#include <stdlib.h>

int *func()

{

int *j = (int *)malloc(sizeof(int));

*j = 20;

return j;
```

```
}
int main()

{

int *ptr = func();

printf ("%d", *ptr);

return 0;

}
```

ANSWER: 20

This is an alternative way of solving Q12.

malloc () is a standard library function in C defined in stdlib.h header file which is used to allocate memory at run time. malloc () returns a generic pointer which indicates that it is a pointer to a region of unknown data type and it must be typecasted with appropriate data type for which , it has allocated the memory. In C, the library function malloc is used to allocate a block of memory on the heap due to which value stored in **j** persists even after the control comes inside main () block. The program accesses this block of memory via a pointer that malloc returns.

Q14. What will be the output of below C code?

```
#include <stdio.h>

int main()

{

int x = 320;

char *ptr = (char *) &x;

printf ("%d", *ptr);

return 0;
```

}

Q15. What will be the output of below C code?

```c
#include <stdio.h>

fun(int x, int y)

{

int *m = &x;

int *n = &y;

if (x > 10)

return m;

else

return n;

}

int main()

{

int *ptr = fun(10, 20);

printf ("%d", *ptr);

return 0;

}
```

ANSWER: Compilation error.

If you observe carefully, you will notice that return type of function fun () is missing but in C, by default, return type of a function in **int** whereas fun () is returning an integer pointer (see last two return statements of fun ()) which contradicts and results into compilation error. To make this code error free just add int * before fun ().

Q16. What will be the output of below C code?

```c
#include <stdio.h>
int main()
{
char *ptr = NULL;
char *p = 0;
if (ptr)
printf ("C");
else
printf ("C++");
if (p)
printf ("Java");
else
printf ("C#");
return 0;
}
```

ANSWER: C++ C#

Both character pointers ptr and p are null pointers. Null pointers don't contain any addresses, thereby making both if () false and we get the desired output.

Q17. What will be the output of below C code?

```c
#include <stdio.h>

int main()
{
printf ("%d %d", sizeof(NULL), sizeof(""));

return 0;

}
```

ANSWER: 2 / 4   1

NULL is a macro in C hence after preprocessing NULL will be replaced by 0 which is an integer and it takes 2/4 bytes of memory. "" (null string) denotes an empty string in C but still contains '\0' (string terminator) which is a character and occupies 1 byte of memory.

Q18. What will be the output of below C code?

```c
#include<stdio.h>

int main()
{
int x = 10;

void *p = &x;

int *ptr = p;

printf ("%d", *ptr);

return 0;

}
```

ANSWER: 10

In C, we can assign the address of any data type to a void pointer without typecasting. Also, a void pointer can be assigned to any pointers. Some compilers may give a warning (like Visual C++). But it's perfectly valid in C.

Q19. What will be the output of below C code?

```
#include <stdio.h>

int main()

{

int x = 2, *ptr;

void *p;

ptr = p = &x;

p++;

ptr++;

printf ("%d %d", *p, *ptr);

return 0;

}
```

ANSWER: Compilation error.

Here, we can increment or decrement pointer **ptr** but no arithmetic operation can be performed on void pointer. To perform arithmetic operations on void pointer, it must be appropriately typecasted.

Q20. What will be the output of below C code?

```
#include <stdio.h>

void func (int *x, int *y)

{

x = y;
```

```
    *x = 4;

}

int m = 1, n = 2;

int main()

{

func (&m, &n);

printf ("%d %d", m, n);

return 0;

}
```

ANSWER: 1 4

Addresses of variable **m** and **n** have been passed to func (). Pointer **x** points to m and pointer **y** points to n. Inside func (), **x** also starts pointing to n and through pointer **x**, value of n has been changed to 4. This is the power of pointer.

Q21. What will be the output of below C code?

```
#include<stdio.h>

int main()

{

int x = 10;

void *ptr = (int *) &x;

printf ("%d", *ptr);

return 0;

}
```

ANSWER: Compile time error (segmentation fault)

In C/C++, void pointers can't be de-referenced. Inside printf (), we have used dereference operator on void pointer which results into compilation error. To compile the program, just typecast the ptr by (int *) and then use dereference operator on it.

Q22. What will be the output of below C code?

```
#include<stdio.h>

int main()

{

int x = 10;

void *ptr = (int *) &x;

printf ("%d", *(int *) ptr);

return 0;

}
```

ANSWER: 10

Q23. What will be the output of below C code?

```
#include <stdio.h>

int main()

{

int *ptr;

*ptr = 20;

printf ("%d", *ptr);

return 0;
```

}

ANSWER: 20

This code works fine but it is a bad way to use pointer **ptr** to store 20. It is so because **ptr** has not been initialized with any memory location. It contains garbage address and storing a value at garbage address is a bad practice in C.

Q24. Is the below C code valid for declaring a null pointer?

int x = 0;

double *ptr = (double *)x;

ANSWER: No. To declare a null pointer, we will have to write

double *ptr = 0 or

double *ptr = (double *)0

Q25. Write a C statement to represent a null pointer in C using **void**?

ANSWER: (void *) 0

Q26. How will you write a C statement in which variable **ptr** is a pointer to a pointer to a pointer to a pointer to a float?

ANSWER: float ****ptr;

Q27. What is the difference between ++*ptr and *ptr++?

ANSWER: Both expressions are different to each other and work in a different way. Both operators- ++ and * (dereference operator) have same precedence and right to left associativity. Hence, ++*ptr increments the value being pointed to by ptr whereas *ptr++ increments the pointer to next memory location of its type, it doesn't increase the value, pointed by ptr.

Note: - ++*ptr can also be written as (*ptr)++ and is equivalent to *ptr = *ptr + 1.

Q28. What will be the output of below C code?

```c
#include <stdio.h>
int func(int x, int *ptr1, int **ptr2)
{
  int y, z;
  **ptr2 += 1;
  z = **ptr2;
  *ptr1 += 2;
  y = *ptr1;
  x += 3;
  return (x + y + z);
}
int main()
{
int x, *y, **z;
x = 2;
y = &x;
z = &y;
printf ("%d", func(x, y, z));
return 0;
}
```

ANSWER: 13

Here, **x** is an integer variable, **y** is a pointer to an integer and **z** is a pointer to an integer pointer (i, e pointer to a pointer). Inside func (), both **ptr1** and

ptr2 is pointing to **x** i, e 2. Variable **x** has been passed by value not by reference hence its value will remain unaffected by the operations being done on **ptr1** and **ptr2**. Rest of the things are simple.

Q29. What will be the output of below C code?

#include <stdio.h>

int i;

void func(void *ptr)

{

int **p;

p = (int **) &ptr;

printf ("%d", **p);

}

int main()

{

void *ptr;

ptr = &i;

func (ptr);

return 0;

}

ANSWER: 0

Think at your own.

Q30. How will you write the prototype of a C function which accepts a pointer to a pointer to a pointer to a char and returns a pointer to a pointer to int?

173

ANSWER: int ** func (char ***);

Q31. What will be the output of below C code?

```c
#include <stdio.h>

void func(int *j)

{

int i = 10;

j = &i;

}

int main()

{

int x = 30;

int *ptr = &x;

func (ptr);

printf ("%d",  *ptr);

return 0;

}
```

ANSWER: 30

In this program, we have passed a local pointer to an integer in func () and collected it in other pointer **j** inside func (). Inside func (), we are trying to assign a new value to pointer **ptr**. But it will not happen because pointer **j** is just a copy of **ptr**, for better understanding you can say that **ptr** was passed as "call by value not call by reference", think over it, you will definitely get what I am trying to say here, so what has been done inside func () will remain to func () scope only. If we want to change a local pointer of one function inside another function, then we must pass pointer to the pointer. By passing the pointer to the pointer, we can change pointer to point to something else.

Q32. What will be the output of below C code?

```
#include <stdio.h>

void func(int **j)

{

int i = 10;

*j = &i;

}

int main()

{

    int x = 30;

    int *ptr = &x;

    func (&ptr);

    printf ("%d", *ptr);

    return 0;

}
```

ANSWER: GARBAGE Value will be printed.

Again we are getting some unexpected output but we will get because we did what has been mentioned in the explanation of Q31, still unexpected output. If you observe carefully then you will see that variable **i** is having **auto** storage class and as soon as control comes out of func () and goes into main (), this variable **i** dies and is no more available and hence we get some garbage value.

Q33. What will be the output of below C code?

```
#include <stdio.h>

void func(int **j)

{

static int i = 10;

*j = &i;

}

int main()

{

int x = 30;

int *ptr = &x;

func (&ptr);

printf ("%d", *ptr);

return 0;

}
```

ANSWER: 10

As we know that **static** variables exist in memory even after functions return. Hence, in this program we will definitely get the expected output i, e 10.

Q34. What will be the output of below C code?

```
# include <stdio.h>

# include <stdlib.h>

void func(int *ptr)

{

ptr = (int *)malloc(sizeof(int));
```

```
}

int main()

{

int *q;

func (q);

*q = 6;

printf ("%d", *q);

return 0;

}
```

ANSWER: Run Time error (Segmentation fault)

Most of the compilers like **Ideone** and **codepad** will give 6 as output but this code will cause an error at run time. Pointer **q** is uninitialized and has been passed to func () as "call by value". Inside func (), we have received a copy of pointer **q** into pointer **ptr** and malloc () has allocated memory for **ptr** not for pointer **q**. Pointer **q** will remain pointing to a random memory location before and after function call. Inside main (), when we will dereference this pointer **q**, program may crash, in some cases leads to run time error. To run this program successfully, pass **q** as "call by reference" i, e pass the address of the pointer (i, e. double pointer).

Note: - Remember on dereferencing a null pointer or an uninitialized pointer in C, will lead to segmentation fault (core dumped) which is a run time error.

Q35. What will be the output of below C code?

```
#include <stdio.h>

int main()

{
```

```
int arr[] = {11, 22, 33, 44, 55};

printf ("%d %d %d", sizeof(arr), sizeof(*arr), sizeof(arr[0]));

return 0;

}
```

ANSWER: 20 4 4 (consider size of integer is 4 bytes)

11	22	33	44	55
65512	65516	65520	65524	65528

This is how array elements are stored in memory. Clearly, elements are stored in consecutive memory locations. Array name always gives the base address of an array; here 65512 (say) is the base address of array **arr**. Hence arr (name of array) is like a pointer which contains the base (starting) address of this array. When array name is used with the **sizeof** operator, it yields total bytes of memory allocated for that particular array. Hence, in our case total 20 bytes of memory have been allocated. When we dereference the name of an array (*array_name), we get the element stored at that position. That is why, (*arr) gives 11. Also using index position, we can access the array elements like arr[i] where i = index position. So, arr [0] will yield 11.

Q36. What will be the output of below C code?

```
#include <stdio.h>

int main()

{

/* suppose base address of array is 65512 */

int arr [] = {11, 22, 33, 44, 55};

printf ("%u %u %u %u", arr, &arr, arr + 1, &arr + 1);

return 0;

}
```

ANSWER: 65512 65512 65514 65532

As we know, mentioning the name of an array yields the base address hence arr yields base address i, e 65512 but, **&arr** also yields the same address, remember, it will, but both are quite different things where **arr** gives the base address, **&arr** gives the address of array of integers. In our case, both are giving the same address but both are different expressions. **arr + 1** will give address of next memory location because when a pointer is incremented, it always points to an immediately next location of its type. Hence, **arr + 1** yield 65514 (next location). Similarly, **&arr + 1** will give the address of next array of 5 integers and that array will have 65532 as its base (starting) address.

Note: - **arr** and **&arr** may refer to same location but they mean two different things.

Q37. What will be the output of below C code?

```c
#include <stdio.h>

int main()

{

int arr[] = {1, 2, 3, 4, 5};

printf ("%d", sizeof(arr) / sizeof(arr[0]));

return 0;

}
```

ANSWER: 5

Remember it. This is a best way for knowing the number of elements in any array. More precisely, you should use sizeof (arr) / sizeof (int) because our array is of **int** type. Now you know what sizeof (arr) and sizeof (arr [0] will yield.

Q38. What will be the output of below C code?

```c
#include <stdio.h>

int main()

{

int arr[10];

printf ("%d", *arr + 1 - *arr + 4);

return 0;

}
```

ANSWER: 5

We know that * (dereference operator) has higher precedence than arithmetic + and − operator. Also, **arr** will yield base address of this uninitialized array. Let's say **arr** yields a value 'y' so our expression inside printf will look like y + 1 − y + 4, and this evaluates to 5.

Q39. What will be the output of below C code?

```c
#include <stdio.h>

int main()

{

int arr[] = {2, 3, 4};

char *ptr = (char *) arr;

printf("%d ", *ptr);

ptr += 1;

printf ("%d", *ptr);

return 0;

}
```

00000010 00000000	3	4
65512	65514	65516

We have declared a **char** pointer **ptr** which points to base address of array **arr**. As we know, decimal 2 will be stored as shown in fig above. Consider INTEL machine (little endian architecture) and 16-bit compiler. So, **ptr** will contain only the first 8-bits i, e 00000010 and hence ***ptr** will give 2. But after incrementing the **ptr** by 1, the pointer will now point to immediately next 8-bits i, e 00000000 and now ***ptr** gives decimal 0.

Note: - A pointer when incremented always points to an immediately next location of its type. Here **ptr** is of char type means it expects a **char** (1 byte) value on dereferencing, so on incrementing it by 1, it will start pointing to next memory location having 1 byte value (8-bits).

Q40. What will be the output of below C code?

```c
#include <stdio.h>

int main()

{
/*suppose base address of arr is 65512 */

int arr[] = {11, 22, 33, 44, 55};

char *ptr = (char *) arr;

/* add a statement here to print 55 using ptr */

return 0;

}
```

ANSWER: printf ("%d", *((int *) ptr + 4));

Pointer **ptr** is of char type so firstly typecast the **ptr** by (int *) and then add 4 but what actually compiler does inside is- it will replace ((int *) ptr + 4) inside printf by 65512 + 4 * 4 which is equivalent to 65528 and hence *(65528) will yield 55.

Note: - To access any element of an array via a pointer, simply do this- ***(base address + index position * sizeof (data type of array))**. Remember if there is a need of typecasting then typecast properly before using above expression. Same thing has been done in this question.

Q41. What will be the output of below C code?

#include <stdio.h>

int main()

{

/* suppose base address of array is 65512 */

int arr[] = {11, 22, 33, 44, 55};

int *ptr = arr;

if (&ptr == &arr)

printf ("True");

else

printf ("Not True");

return 0;

}

ANSWER: Not True

11	22	33	44	55
65512	65516	65520	65524	65528

7441

Clearly, &ptr = 7441,

&arr = 65512

So, &ptr! = &arr

Rest of the things are simple to interpret.

Q42. What will be the output of below C code?

```c
#include <stdio.h>

int main()

{

/* suppose base address of array is 65512 */

int arr[] = {11, 22, 33, 44, 55};

int *ptr = arr;

if (ptr == &arr)

printf("True");

else

printf ("Not True");

return 0;

}
```

ANSWER: True

Reason is obvious. Try to understand at your own.

Q43. What will be the output of below C code?

```c
#include <stdio.h>
```

```c
int main()

{

/* consider int is of 4 bytes */

int arr[] = {1, 2, 3, 4, 5};

int *ptr = arr;

printf ("%d %d", sizeof(arr), sizeof(ptr));

return 0;

}
```

ANSWER: 20 4

Here **ptr** is a pointer which takes 4 bytes of space in memory.

Q44. What will be the output of below C code?

```c
#include <stdio.h>

int main()

{

int arr[] = {11, 22, 33, 44, 55};

int i;

for (i = 0; i <= 4; ++i)

{

printf ("%d", *arr);

++arr;

}

return 0;
```

}

ANSWER: Compilation error- Lvalue required in main ().

As I have already mentioned that name of an array holds the base of an array and we can treat it as a pointer type but name of an array is implicitly **const** type in nature and we can't perform post/pre increment or decrement operation on the name of an array. In simple words, name of an array always holds (refer) to the base address of an array and it is not possible to change its content directly. But you can assign the content to another pointer of same type and then can do post/pre increment or decrement operation.

Q45. What will be the output of below C code?

#include<stdio.h>

int main()

{

/* suppose base address of array is 65512 */

 int arr[] = {1, 2, 3, 4, 5, 6};

 int *ptr = (int*)(&arr+1);

 printf ("%d", *(ptr - 1));

 return 0;

}

ANSWER: 6

1	2	3	4	5	6
65512	65516	65520	65524	65528	65532

As we know, in this case **&arr** will give the address of an array of ints. So, adding 1 to it will give us the address of next array of ints starting from 65536 memory location i, e base address of this new array will be 65536. Hence **ptr** will contain 65536 and when we subtract 1 from **ptr**, it will come back to

185

65532 location because *(ptr − 1) is actually *(65536 − 1 * 4) which is equal to *(65532) and value contained at this location is nothing but 6.

Q46. What will be the output of below C code?

```
#include <stdio.h>

int main()

{

int arr[] = {10, 20, 30};

printf ("%d %d %d %d %d %d", 0[arr], arr[0], 1[arr], arr[1], 2[arr], arr[2]);

return 0;

}
```

ANSWER: 10 10 20 20 30 30

In C, we know that on mentioning the name of array, we get its base address and on doing ***arr** or **arr[i]**, we get the element stored at that location. But, in fact, what compiler does internally is worth knowing. Compilers internally coverts ***arr** or **arr[i]** to ***(arr + i)**.Hence arr[i], *(arr + i), i[arr], *(i + arr) are same and will give same answer. Do remember, the Note mentioned below Q40. Did you?

Q47. What will be the output of below C code? Try this on 16-bit compiler?

```
#include <stdio.h>

int main()

{

int a[]={1,2,3,4,5,6,7,8,9,10};

int *p = a;

p = (int *) (((char*) a) + 1);
```

```
printf ("%d", *p);

return 0;

}
```

ANSWER: 2 (On 16-bit compiler).

Q48. What will be the output of below C code?

```
#include <stdio.h>

int main()

{

int a[]={1, 2, 3, 4, 5},i;

int *p = (a + 3);

char *s = ((char *)p) + 1;

int t=*((char *)p);

*((char *) p) = *s;

*s = t;

for (i = 0; i< 5; i++)

printf ("%d", a [i]);

return 0;

}
```

ANSWER: Try to figure out the working of this program.

Q49. In C, on mentioning the name of an array, we get the base address of that array. Is it true in all contexts?

ANSWER: No, it is not true in all contexts. It's true, on mentioning the array name; we get the base address because internally array name gets decomposed automatically into a pointer. This decomposition doesn't happen in below two cases:-

1. When array name is used with **sizeof ()** operator.

2. When array name is the operand of **&** (address-of-operator).

Note: - In C, if we pass an array as an argument to a function then, actually base address gets passed and array name also gets decomposed into a pointer.

Q50. What will be the output of below C code?

```c
#include <stdio.h>

void print(int *arr)

{

int size = sizeof(arr) / sizeof(arr[0]);

int i;

for (i = 0; i <size; ++i)

printf("%d ", arr[i]);

}

int main()

{

int a[] = {11, 22, 33, 44, 55};

print (a);

return 0;

}
```

ANSWER: 11

Shocked..!!! Only 11, but this code will print only 11. It is so because whenever array name is passed an argument to a function, array name gets decayed into a pointer. Hence, **arr** inside print () is a pointer not the name of an array now. Both sizeof (arr) and sizeof (arr [0]) will give 4 and hence variable **size** contains 1 and for loop executes for one time only.

Note: - Do remember about this behaviour.

Q51. What will be the output of below C code?

```
#include <stdio.h>

int main()

{

int arr[] = {1, 2, 3, 4, 5};

int x, y, z;

x = ++arr[0];

y = arr[0]++;

z = arr[++x];

printf ("%d %d %d", x, y, z);

return 0;

}
```

ANSWER: 3 2 4

Apply the concept of pre-increment and post-increment to get the output.

Q52. What is the difference between these two declarations- int *ptr [5] and int (*ptr) [5]?

ANSWER: **int *ptr [5]** means **ptr** is an array of five integer pointers, means array elements are nothing but pointers to integers whereas **int (*ptr)**

[5] means **ptr** is a pointer to an array of five integers. We will discover more on several complicated declaration in C in our coming chapter.

Q53. Do we have bound checking in C?

ANSWER: No, we don't have bound checking in C. In computer programming, bounds checking are any method of detecting whether a variable is within some bounds before it is used. It is usually used to ensure that a number fits into a given type (range checking), or that a variable being used as an array index is within the bounds of the array (index checking). Data entered with a script exceeding the array size will be placed in memory outside the array or at some random location and this will lead to unpredictable result.

Q54. What will be the output of below C code?

```
#include <stdio.h>

int main()

{

/* suppose base address of array is 65512 */

int arr[] = {11, 22, 33, 44, 55};

int *ptr1, *ptr2;

ptr1 = &arr[1];

ptr2 = &arr[4];

printf ("%d %d", ptr2 - ptr1, *ptr2 - *ptr1);

return 0;

}
```

ANSWER: 3 33

Clearly **ptr1** and **ptr2** point to 65516 and 65528 respectively whereas ***ptr1** and ***ptr2** contain 22 and 55 respectively. Now, the expression **ptr2 − ptr1** would give 3 not 12. This is so because **ptr1** and **ptr2** are pointing to locations that are three integers apart. Remember this. The expression ***ptr2 − *ptr1** will simply give the difference of the values stored at these locations i, e (55 − 22 = 33).

Q55. What will be the output of below C code?

```
#include <stdio.h>

int main()

{

/* suppose base address of array is 65512 */

int arr[] = {11, 22, 33, 44, 55};

int *ptr;

for (ptr = arr + 4; ptr >= arr; --ptr)

printf ("%d", arr[ptr – arr]);

return 0;

}
```

ANSWER: 55 44 33 22 11

11	22	33	44	55
65512	65516	65520	65524	65528

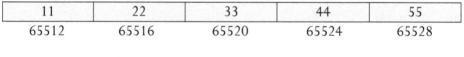

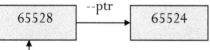

In loop, **ptr** has been initialized with the address of last element i, e with 65528. Since 65528 >= 65512, printf () gets executed and expression **arr[65528 − 65512]** is equivalent to **arr[4]** not **arr[16]**, why? Go through

Q54 and **arr[4]** is nothing but 55. In the same way, for () loop runs till **ptr >= arr** is true.

Q56. What will be the output of below C code?

```
#include <stdio.h>

int main()

{

int arr[] = {11, 22, 33, 44, 55};

int *ptr = arr + 4;

int j = 0;

for (; j <= 4; j++)

printf ("%d", ptr[-j]);

return 0;

}
```

ANSWER: 55 44 33 22 11

This is not a new type of question. But focus on expression **ptr[-j]**, this nothing but ***(ptr − j)**, this how compiler interprets it internally. Initially, **j** is 0 and **ptr** is pointing to 65528 location hence ***(ptr − j)** evaluates to ***(65528 − 0)** or ***(65528 − 0 * sizeof(int))** and value at this location is 55. Next time we will have ***(65528 − 1 * sizeof(int))** i, e ***(65528 − 4)** i, e ***(65524)** which contains 44. Again, ***(65528 − 2 * sizeof(int))** i, e ***(65528 − 8)** i, e ***(65520)** and value contained at this location is 33. Likewise, we will get 22 and 11.

Q57. Can we have a variable sized array in C?

ANSWER: Yes. According to C99 standard, a variable sized array is possible in C but unlike the normal arrays, variable sized arrays cannot be initialized. Consider the below C code:-

```c
#include <stdio.h>

int main()

{

int SIZE = 2;

int arr[SIZE][SIZE] ;

int i, j;

for (i = 0; i < SIZE; ++i)

{

    for (j = 0; j < SIZE; ++j)

    {

        /* some codes here */

    }

    printf("\n");

}

return 0;

}
```

Above code will work fine on a C99 compatible compilers. But the following fails with compilation error. See how?

```c
#include <stdio.h>

int main()
```

```
{
    int SIZE = 2;
    int arr[SIZE][SIZE] = {0};  // we can't initialize a variable sized array.
    int i, j;
    for (i = 0; i < SIZE; ++i)
    {
        for (j = 0; j < SIZE; ++j)
        {
            /* some codes here */
        }
        printf ("\n");
    }
    return 0;
}
```

Program fails to compile because according to standard, variable-sized object may not be initialized.

Q58. What will be the output of below C code?

```
#include <stdio.h>
int main()
{
    int arr[][2] = {
                    {103011, 11},
                    {103022, 22},
```

{103033, 33},

{103044, 44}

};

int i;

for (i = 0; i <= 3; ++i)

printf ("%d ", arr[i]);

return 0;

}

ANSWER: 6442 6450 6458 6466

103011	11	103022	22	103033	33	103044	44
6442	6446	6450	6454	6458	6462	6466	6470

The figure clearly represents how the elements of a 2-D array are stored in memory. Remember, there is nothing like rows and columns in memory. In memory whether it is a 1-D array or a 2-D array the elements are always stored in consecutive memory locations. Hence **arr[0][0]** means 103011, **arr[0][1]** means 11 and likewise for other elements. In fact a 2-D array is nothing but a collection of 1-D array placed one after another. Let's go in more depth of 2-D array because I personally believe many students don't have so many concepts as far as 2-D array is concerned. Read this carefully because explanations given here will help you a lot in solving many questions based on 2-D array.

In this program we have declared a 2-D array: - int arr[][2]; Array **arr** can be considered as setting up a 1-D array of four elements, each of which is a 1-D

array of two elements. We can access (refer) to each of the element using a single subscript. Hence, **arr[0]** refers to the zeroth element, **arr[1]** refers to first element and so on but in case of a 2-D array, zeroth element is nothing but a 1-D array hence printf **("%d", arr[0])** will give base address of the array which is present at this location because as we know that on mentioning 1-D array gives its base address. Similarly, **arr[1], arr[2] ....arr[i]** all will give the base address of the 1-D array and it is also clear from the output. In C, the name of a 2-D array is also treated as a pointer which points to zeroth element of 2-D array. Hence expression **(arr + 0)** gives us the address of the 0th element of 2-D array and on dereferencing this expression i, e ***(arr + 0)** will give the 0th element which is nothing but a 1-D array. So, ***(arr + 0)** gives the base address of the 0th 1-D array which is 6442 as shown in figure. Similarly, **arr[1], arr[2],....arr[i]** are nothing but ***(arr + 1), *(arr + 2)** and so on. Now if have observed carefully then you will come to know that we are now able to reach each individual row of **arr**. So using these addresses we can access each elements of 1-D array using pointer notation. We know **arr[1][1]** gives 22 but we can also access 22 in a different way because we know **arr[1]** would give 6450, the address of 1st 1-D array. Obviously, on doing (6450 + 1) would give 6454 or in other way **arr[1] + 1** would give 6454 and hence ***(arr[1] + 1)** would give 22 which is stored at this location. Also, in ***(arr[1] + 1)** is nothing but ***(*(arr + 1) + 1)**. Hence, do remember that all below expressions refer to same element-

1. arr[1][1]

2.*(arr[1] + 1)

3. *(*(arr + 1) +1)

Note:- Do remember what I have discussed here because it is not a text-book but still I tried to give you every concept of 2-D array in brief.

Q59. Given an array whose base address is 1000 and the array is arr[5][4] then what will be the correct address of arr[4][3]?

ANSWER: There is a formula for such types of questions-

(base address + row no * number of columns + column no.)

For our question we will have- (1000 + 4 * 4 + 3) = (1000 + 19 * 4) = (1076). Hence address of arr[4][3] will be 1076.

Q60. What will be the output of below C code?

```
#include <stdio.h>

int main()

{

/* suppose base address of arr is 65512 */

int main()

{

int arr[][3] = {
                {1, 2, 3},
                {4, 5, 6},
                {7, 8, 9}
             };
printf ("%u %u %u ", arr, arr + 1, &arr + 1);

return 0;

}
```

ANSWER: 65512 65524 65548

Since **arr** is a pointer, pointing to 0th element of the array which is a 1-D array hence we get 65512 as our first output. Also we know that when a pointer is incremented or decremented then it starts pointing to an immediately next location of its type and **arr** is a pointer to a 1-D array type then on doing **arr + 1** we get the base address of 1st 1-D array i, e 65524 and this is our second output. We also know that **&arr + 1** will give the address of next 2-D array of 3 rows and 2 columns. So we get 65548 as our third output.

Q61. What will be the output of below C code?

#include <stdio.h>

int main()

{

/* suppose base address of array is 65512 */

int arr[3][2] = {4, 8, 12, 16, 20, 24};

printf ("%d %d", *(arr + 1)[1], **(arr + 2));

return 0;

}

ANSWER: 20 20

The given 2-D array can be also written as-

int arr[3][2] = {

                {4, 8},

                {12, 16},

                {20, 24}

            };

Here, for better understanding, suppose ***(arr + 1)** is **a** then ***(arr + 1)[1]** will be **a[1]** i, e ***(a +1)**. Now, replace **a** by ***(arr + 1)** then we get ***(*(arr + 1) + 1))** is again equivalent to ***(*(arr + 2))** which again equivalent to ***(arr[2])** which is finally equal to ***(arr[2] + 0)** and value contained at this location is 20. Expression ****(arr + 2)** is equivalent to ***(*(arr + 2))** i, e ***(arr[2])** i, e ***(arr[2] + 0)** and value contained at this location is also 20.

Q62. What will be the output of below C code?

```c
#include <stdio.h>
int main()
{
/* suppose base address of array is 65512 */
int arr[][3] = {
            {1, 2, 3},
            {4, 5, 6},
            {7, 8, 9}
        };
printf ("%u %u %d %d", arr[0] + 1, *arr + 1, *(a[0] + 1), *(*(a + 0) + 1));
return 0;
}
```

ANSWER: 65516 65516 2 2

Nothing is new here. All concepts have already been discussed. Go through the outputs and do at you own.

Q63. What will be the output of below C code?

```c
#include <stdio.h>
#define ROW 10
#define COL 20
int main()
{
int (*ptr)[ROW][COL];
```

```c
printf ("%d %d ", sizeof(ptr), sizeof(*ptr));

printf ("%d %d", sizeof(**ptr), sizeof(***ptr));

return 0;

}
```

ANSWER: 4 800 80 4

Here, **ptr** is a pointer to a 2-D array of 10 rows and 20 columns. **sizeof(ptr)** will give 4 as expected. But **sizeof(*ptr)** gives 800 but how? Actually **(*ptr)** is nothing but name of an array i,e on dereferencing **ptr**, compiler comes to know about its type of object. In the present case, it is an array of array of integers. So, it prints ROW*COL*sizeof(int) i, e 10*20*4 = 800. Similarly, **(**ptr)** is nothing but a single 1-D array type which contains 20 elements of **int** type. Hence **sizeof(**ptr)** gives 80. Remember, when array name is used with **sizeof ()**, then sizeof () returns the total number of bytes allocated for that array. And lastly **sizeof(***ptr)** gives 4 because ***ptr is an integer located at (0, 0) of 2-D array.

Q64. What will be the output of below C code?

```c
#include <stdio.h>

int main()

{

/* suppose base address of array is 65512 */

int arr[3][3] = {
                  {1, 2, 3},
                  {4, 5, 6},
                  {7, 8, 9}
                };
```

printf ("%u %u %d", arr, arr[1], arr[1][1]);

return 0;

}

ANSWER: 65512 65524 5

Output is obvious, no need of explanations. All concepts have already been discussed. Still you are having problem, kindly go through previous questions.

Q65. What will be the output of below C code?

#include <stdio.h>

int main()

{

/* suppose base address of array is 65512 */

int arr[][3] = {

                {1, 2, 3},

                {4, 5, 6},

                {7, 8, 9}

            };

int *ptr = arr;   /* need some modification */

printf ("%u %d %d", arr[2], ptr[2], *(ptr + 2));

return 0;

}

ANSWER: Compilation error- "cannot convert 'int (*)[3]' to 'int*' in initialization".

Compilers like Ideone & codepad will not give any compilation issue but Dev C++ and Visual C++ will give compilation error and it should, because pointers **ptr** and **arr** are of completely different type, they are not compatible to each other until proper typecasting has not been done. As we know, **ptr** is a pointer to an integer whereas **arr** is a pointer to the zeroth element of 2-D array which is a 1-D array. Clearly both types are different. Hence, to compile our program just typecast **arr** with **(int *)** and output of program will be- 65512 3 3.

arr[2] gives base address of 2nd 1-D array which is 65512. **ptr[2]** is nothing but ***(ptr + 2)** which gives 3 because *(ptr + 2) is equivalent to ***(65512 + 2 * sizeof(int))** i, e ***(65512 + 8)** i, e ***(65520)** and 3 is contained at this location.

Q66. In C, when the name of a 1-D array is passed to a function, it decays into a pointer of array type but if the name of a 2-D array is passed then what will it decay into when passed to a function?

ANSWER: It will decay into a pointer to an array. Remember, it will not decay into a pointer to pointer.

Q67. Write the three prototype declarations of a function which accepts a 2-D array as a parameter?

ANSWER: Consider, ROW stands for number of rows in 2-D array and COL stands for number of columns and ROW = 4 & COL = 4

1. void func_type1(int *ptr, int ROW, int COL);

2. void func_type2(int (*ptr)[4], int ROW, int COL);

3. void func_type3(int ptr[][4], int ROW, int COL);

Expression	Meaning
int *ptr	ptr is a pointer to an integer
int (*ptr)[4]	ptr is a pointer to an array of 4 integers
int ptr[][4]	ptr is a pointer to an array of 4 integers

Q68. What will be the output of below C code?

```c
#include <stdio.h>
#define ROW 4
#define COL 4
/* func1 modifies the given array */
void func1(int arr[][COL])
{
  arr++;
  arr[1][3] = 'A';
  arr++;
  arr[1][3] = 'B';
}
/* func2 prints 2-D array */
void func2(int arr[][COL])
{
int i, j;
for (i = 0; i < ROW; i++)
{
for (j = 0; j < COL; j++)
printf("%d ", arr[i][j]);
printf("\n");
}
```

```
}
int main()
{
int arr[ROW][COL] = {
                    {1, 2, 3, 4},
                    {5, 6, 7, 8},
                    {9, 10, 11, 12},
                    {13, 14, 15, 16}
                    };
func1(arr);
printf ("2-D array after modifications:\n");
func2(arr);
return 0;
}
```

ANSWER: 2-D array after modifications:

1 2 3 4

5 6 7 8

9 10 11 65

13 14 15 66

Here inside func1 () we are modifying the 2-D array. When **arr++** is executed, **arr** starts pointing to next row and hence **arr[1][3]** refers to 12 in our original matrix which has been replaced by ASCII value of 'A'. Similarly when **arr++** is done second time then **arr[1][3]** refers to 16 but has been replaced by ASCII value of 'B'.

Q69. What will be the output of below C code?

```c
#include <stdio.h>
int main()
{
/* suppose base address of array is 65512 */
int arr[][4] = {
                {1, 2, 3, 4},
                {5, 6, 7, 8},
                {9, 5, 8, 0}
               };
int *ptr;
int (*p)[4];
ptr = (int *)arr;
p = arr;
printf ("%u %u", ptr, p);
++ptr;
++p;
printf ("%u %u", ptr, p);
return 0;
}
```

ANSWER: 65512 65512 65516 65528

No need to explain the output now. We did a lot of problems on 1-D and 2-D array. Let's switch to another interesting topic- "Array of pointers".

Q70. What will be the output of below C code?

#include <stdio.h>

int main()

{

int x, y, z;

x = 5;

y =10;

z = 15;

int *arr[3] = {&x, &y, &z};

printf("%d", *arr[*arr[1] - 10]);

return 0;

}

ANSWER: 5

Go through the diagram drawn below for better understanding.

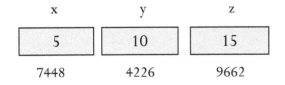

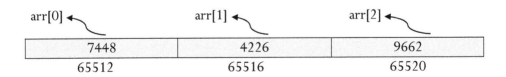

Clearly, ***arr[1]** is equal to ***(4226)** i, e 10 hence expression ***arr[*arr[1]** **– 10]** is now equivalent to ***arr[10 – 10]** i, e ***arr[0]** which is equivalent to ***(7448)** and value stored at this location is 5.

Q71. What will be the output of below C code?

```c
#include <stdio.h>

int main()

{

static int arr[] = {11, 22, 33, 44, 55};

static int *ptr[] = {arr + 4, arr + 3, arr + 2, arr + 1, arr};

printf ("%u %d %d", ptr, *ptr, **ptr);

return 0;

}
```

ANSWER: 7442 65528 11

arr[]:

11	22	33	44	55
65512	65516	65520	65524	65528

ptr[]:

65528	65524	65520	65516	65512
7442	7446	7450	7454	7458

Here **ptr** is an array of pointers to integers. As you can see in the figure, array **ptr** contains the address of each element of array **arr** and clearly, **ptr** contains 7442, base address of array **ptr**. Rest of the things are simple because we know how **ptr**, ***ptr** and ****ptr** works.

Q72. What will be the output of below C code?

```c
#include <stdio.h>
int main()
{
static int arr[] = {11, 22, 33, 44, 55};
static int *ptr[] = {arr, arr + 1, arr + 2, arr + 3, arr + 4};
int **q = ptr;
**++q;
printf ("%d %d %d", **q, q – ptr, *q – arr);
return 0;
}
```

ANSWER: 22 1 1

arr[]:

11	22	33	44	55
65512	65516	65520	65524	65528

ptr[]:

65512	65516	65520	65524	6552
7442	7446	7450	7454	7458

The expression **++q will first increment pointer q to point 7446 memory location. Then **(7446) would yield 2, which is ignored since it has not been assigned to any variable. Now, pointer ptr is pointing to 7446 and hence **q inside printf () gives 22. The expression **(q − ptr)** is nothing but (7446 − 7442) which gives 1 because these locations are 1 integer apart. Did you remember, how? Similarly, expression **(*q − arr)** is **(65516 − 65512)** which also gives 1 because both addresses are again 1 integer apart.

Note:- For solving such problems, you should first draw the memory arrangement diagram and then try to evaluate the given expressions. I am sure you will get a better concept and can proceed further without any problem. Remember this is not the end of this chapter, it's just a beginning, and a lot of problems will be covered in next edition of this book.

Chapter-8

Strings In C

Q1. What will be the output of below C code?

```c
#include <stdio.h>

int main()

{

char str[] = "Hello";

int i;

for (i = 0; str[i]; ++i)

printf ("%c %c %c %c\n", str[i], *(str + i), i[str], *(i + str));

return 0;

}
```

ANSWER: H H H H

         e e e e

         l l l l

         o o o o

str[]:

H	e	l	l	o	'\0'
4001	4002	4003	4004	4005	4006

All expressions like- **str[i]**, **i[str]**, ***(str + i)**, ***(i + str)** used inside printf () are just various ways to refer the elements of the string **str**. As you can see, all elements of a string are stored in contiguous memory location. '\0' is a special character, known as "null character" whose ASCII value is 0 and signifies the end of a string. Every string in C must terminate with null character ('\0') otherwise the string will be merely a collection of strings. Notice in **for** () loop, there is an expression **str[i]** which tests whether condition is true or false. If **str[i] != 0** then **for** () loop continues and print each character of string 4 times. **for** () loop gets terminated when a "null character" ('\0') is found and then **str[i]** becomes false (0).

Q2. What will be the output of below C code?

```
#include <stdio.h>

int main()

{

char str[] = "Hello";

char *ptr = "Java";

printf ("%d %d", sizeof(str), sizeof(ptr));

return 0;

}
```

ANSWER: 6 4

sizeof(str) will give 6 because we know that when an array name is used with **sizeof** (), we get the total bytes allocated for the array. Array **str** contains- 'H', 'e', 'l', 'l', 'o' and '\0' and all of these characters are 1 byte long in C hence, total 6 bytes of memory. **ptr** is just a simple **char** pointer which takes 4 bytes.

Note:- If we have a declaration say, char str[20] = "Hello C"; then in this case sizeof(str) will return 20 not 8. It's because **str** has been declared to hold 20 characters and compiler has already allocated 20 bytes of memory. Because we have used only 8 bytes so rest of the 12 bytes go in waste.

Q3. What will be the output of below C code?

```c
#include <stdio.h>

int main()
{
printf ("%d %d %d", sizeof('2'), sizeof("2"), sizeof(2));

return 0;

}
```

ANSWER: 1 2 4

Here, '2' is a character which is 1 byte long. "2" is a string which also "null character" ('\0') hence 2 bytes for each character. 2 is an integer which takes 4 bytes on 32-bit system.

Q4. What will be the output of below C code?

```c
#include <stdio.h>

int main()
{
char str1[] = "Concepts In C";

char str2[] = "Concepts In C";

if (str1 == str2)

printf ("Both strings are equal");

else

printf ("Both strings are not equal");

return 0;
```

}

ANSWER: Both strings are not equal

Both strings are located at different memory locations. **str1** and **str2** are completely two different arrays hence their base addresses would be always different. So, **str1 != str2** and hence **else** gets executed.

Q5. What will be the output of below C code?

#include <stdio.h>

int main()

{

printf (6 + "Hello World");

return 0;

}

ANSWER: World

Inside **printf** (), we have actually passed the base address of string "Hello World" + 6. Suppose base address of this array is- **65512** hence **(65512 + 6 *1) = (65518)** gets passed to **printf** () and at this memory location **65518**, character 'W' is stored. So starting from address of 'W', **printf** () prints all characters upto the end of the string.

Q6. What will be the output of below C code?

#include <stdio.h>

int main()

{

printf ("%c", "abcdefgh"[5]);

```c
return 0;

}
```

ANSWER: f

Suppose base address of string "abcdefgh" is 65512 hence expression "abcdefgh"[5] is nothing but ***(65512 + 5 * sizeof(char)) = *(65517)** and at this memory location character 'f' is stored which gets printed by **printf** ().

Q7. What will be the output of below C code?

```c
#include <stdio.h>

int main()

{

printf ("%c", 7["Concepts In C"]);

return 0;

}
```

ANSWER: s

This question is same as that of Q6.

Q8. What will be the output of below C code?

```c
#include <stdio.h>

int main()

{

char str[] = "Hello World";

char *ptr = "Hello World";
```

```
printf ("%d %d", sizeof(*str), sizeof(*ptr));

return 0;

}
```

ANSWER: 1 1

Q9. What is the difference between the following two declarations?

```
char str[] = "Concepts In C";

char *ptr = "Concepts In C";
```

ANSWER: Here **str** is an array when initialized with a double quoted string and array size is not specified, compiler automatically allocates one extra space for "null character" ('\0'). Also if str[] is an **auto** variable then string is stored in stack segment, if it's a **global** or **static** variable then stored in data segment of RAM. You can change the individual characters of array but the address of the array will remain same i, e you can't force the **str** to point to some other locations otherwise it will lead to compilation error.

On the other hand, **ptr** is a pointer, initialized to point to a constant string. Remember, when string value is directly assigned to a pointer, in most of the compilers, it is stored in a read only block (generally in data segment) of RAM but pointer **ptr** is stored in a read-write memory. You can change **ptr** to point some other locations but can't change the value stored at that memory location, pointed by pointer **ptr**. If this happens, it will lead to compilation error.

Q10. What will be the output of below C code?

```
#include <stdio.h>

char * func()

{
```

```c
char str[] = "Let's learn C again";

return (str);

}

int main()

{

printf ("%s", func());

return 0;

}
```

ANSWER: Nothing will be printed.

As explained in Q9, string is stored in stack frame of function func() and as soon as func() returns, the string gets lost from memory because **str** is having **auto** storage class. If we have **static** qualifier before array **str**, then "Let's learn C again", will be printed on console.

Q11. #include <stdio.h>

```c
char * func()

{

char *str = "Let's learn C again";

return (str);

}

int main()

{

printf ("%s", func());
```

return 0;

}

ANSWER: Let's learn C again

The program works perfectly fine as the string is stored in the data segment and the string will remain alive even after the func () returns back to main().

Q12. What will be the output of below C code?

```c
#include <stdio.h>

char *func()

{

int len = 6;

char *str = (char *) malloc(sizeof(char) * len);

*(str + 0) = 'H';

*(str + 1) = 'e';

*(str + 2) = 'l';

*(str + 3) = 'l';

*(str + 4) = 'o';

*(str + 5) = '\0';

return str;

}

int main()

{
```

printf ("%s", func());

return 0;

}

ANSWER: Hello

malloc () allocates memory in heap segment of memory (RAM). Hence, program works perfectly fine as the string is stored in heap segment and data stored in heap segment persists even after func () returns back to main().

Q13. What will be the output of below C code?

#include <stdio.h>

char *func()

{

return ("Hello");

}

int main()

{

printf ("%s", func() + printf ("Let's learn C"));

return 0;

}

ANSWER: Some string starting with Let's learn C

Here function **func** () is returning pointer to a **char**. Also **printf ("Let's learn C")** returns 13 after printing "Let's learn C". Hence, expression inside outer **printf** () reduces to **("Hello" + 13)** which is nothing but base address of string literal "Hello" displaced by 13 characters. Hence, the expression ["Hello" + 13] returns garbage data when printed via **%s** specifier till it finds '\0'.

Q14. What will be the output of below C code?

```c
#include <stdio.h>

int main()

{

char str[4] = "Java";

printf ("%d %s", sizeof(str), str);

return 0;

}
```

ANSWER: 4 GARBAGE VALUE

Here, size of array is fixed i, e 4 but to be a valid string in C, a string must be terminated by '\0. In this program, we have set 4 bytes of memory but actual valid string will take 5 bytes (1 byte extra for '\0') and this is missing. So **sizeof(str)** gives 4 in C whereas **%s** prints a garbage value till it doesn't find a null character because given string is not null ('\0') terminated. This code is will run without any error/warning but it is perfectly invalid in C++. Do remember this one.

Q15. What will be the output of below C code?

```c
#include <stdio.h>

int main()

{

char *ptr = "Java";
```

```
printf ("%s", *&*&*&ptr);

return 0;

}
```

ANSWER: Java

No need to be afraid of ***&*&*&**. We can use as many of ***&*&*&....*&** before **ptr** because **&ptr** yields the address of pointer **ptr** not the content of **ptr**. On dereferencing, **(*&ptr)** yields the base address of string constant "Java" which gets printed by **printf** () using **%s** which need only base address to start with.

Q16. What will be the output of below C code?

```
#include <stdio.h>

int main()

{

char *str = "%d\n";    /* base address of array is 7004 */

++str;

++str;

printf (str - 2, 100);

return 0;

}
```

ANSWER: 100

Initially, **str** is pointing to **'%'** and afterwards it has been incremented twice due to which **str** now points to '\n'. Inside **printf** (), expression **(str - 2)** evaluates to **(7006 - 2 * 1) = (7004)** which again contains '%' and finally **(str - 2)** gets replaced by **"%d\n"** which prints 100.

Q17. What will be the output of below C code?

```c
#include <stdio.h>

int func(char *ptr1)

{

char *ptr2 = ptr1;

while (*++ptr1);

return (ptr1 - ptr2);

}

int main()

{

char *str = "Concepts In C";

printf ("%d", func(str));

return 0;

}
```

ANSWER: 13

Inside **func** (), **ptr1** has been incremented until '\0' is not found. Firstly, **++** will increment the **ptr** then dereference operator **(*)**, dereferences **ptr** to check the value, if loop gets true, then loop executes again otherwise loop becomes false (in case of getting '\0') and **func** () returns the difference between **ptr1** and **ptr2**. In our case difference is 13. Assuming char takes 1 byte.

Q18. What will be the output of below C code?

```c
#include <stdio.h>

int main()

{

char str[] = "Java Perl and Lisp";  /* base address of array is 7004 */

printf ("%c\n", *(&str[3]));

printf ("%s\n", str + 5);

printf ("%s\n", str);

printf ("%s\n", (str + 14));

printf ("%u", str);

return 0;

}
```

ANSWER: a

Perl and Lisp

Java Perl and Lisp

Lisp

7004

First **printf** () prints the 3rd character of the given string **str**. Since expression **&(str[3])** yields the address of 3rd character which gets printed by **printf** () on dereferencing this memory location. As the base address of given string is 7004, hence expression **(str + 5)** yields the address of character 'p' which is nothing but **(7004 + 5 * sizeof(char)) = (7009)** and this address is passed to **printf** () and using **%s**, all characters starting from this location are printed until '\0' is not found. Similarly, expressions **str** and **(str + 14)** works. Do this at your own. Last **printf** () prints the base address of the given string which is 7004. This base address may vary for your compiler, I have chosen 7004 for the sake of convenience.

Q19. What will be the output of below C code?

#include <stdio.h>

int main()

{

void *vptr;

char ch = 82, *ptr = "RAMBO";

int i = 65;

vptr = &ch;

printf ("%c", *(char *)vptr);

vptr = &i;

printf ("%c", *(int *)vptr);

vptr = ptr;

printf ("%s", (char *)vptr + 2);

return 0;

}

ANSWER: RAMBO

In this program, **vptr** is a void pointer. Initially, **vptr** has been assigned the address of character 'R' also inside first **printf** () **vptr** has been typecasted into **char** type, and it is necessary because **void** can't be de-referenced until typecasted properly. Hence first **printf** () prints 'R' because now **vptr** contains the address of 'R'. Same concept applies for second **printf** () which prints 'A' using properly typecasted **void** pointer **vptr**. Now, the expression **(char *)vptr + 2** in third **printf** () gives the address of 3rd character of given string which is 'M' and hence **%s** keeps printing all characters starting from 'M' until null character ('\0') is not found i, e it prints MBO and hence our final output is- RAMBO.

Q20. What will be the output of below C code?

```
#include <stdio.h>

int main()

{

char str[] = {64, 64, 64, 64, 64};

char *ptr = str;

int j;

for (j = 0; j <= 4; ++j)

{

printf ("%c ", *ptr);

++ptr;

}

return 0;

}
```

ANSWER: @ @ @ @ @

In this program, **str** is a char array but we are storing an integer value for each 5 elements of **str[]**. But here 64 is the ASCII value of a character and that character corresponding this ASCII is actually gets stored inside **str[]**. Pointer **ptr** is assigned the base address of **str[]**. Finally **for** () loop prints each character which is nothing but a special character @.

Now try this one at your own.

Q21. What will be the output of below C code?

```c
#include <stdio.h>

int main()

{

char str[] = {48, 48, 48, 48, 48};

char *ptr = str;

int j;

for (j = 0; j <= 4; ++j)

{

if (*ptr)

{

printf ("%c ", *ptr);

++ptr;

}

return 0;

}
```

ANSWER: 0 0 0 0 0 0

Q22. What will be the output of below C code?

```c
#include <stdio.h>

int main()

{

char str[] = "GATE2014";

char *ptr = str;

printf ("%s", ptr + ptr[3] - ptr[1]);

return 0;

}
```

ANSWER: 2014

ptr[3] = ASCII value of E which is 69.

ptr[1] = ASCII value of A which is 65.

Hence, ptr[3] - ptr[1] = (69 - 65) = 4

Clearly, final expression inside **printf** () will be **(ptr + 4)** which is the base address of "2014" and this string gets printed by **%s** format specifier.

Q23. What will be the output of below C code?

```c
#include <stdio.h>

int main()

{

char str1[] = "%d %c";

char str2[] = "Umbrella";  /* base address is 7004 */
```

```c
printf (str1, 0[str2], 2[str2 + 0]);

return 0;

}
```

ANSWER: 85 b

The **printf** () statement is actually **printf ("%d %c", *("Umbrella" + 0), *(2 + "Umbrella" + 0)**. Clearly, **%d** prints the ASCII value of 'U' which is 85 whereas **%c** prints the character located at ***(7004 + 2 * sizeof(char))** which nothing but 'b'.

Q24. What will be the output of below C code?

```c
#include <stdio.h>

int main()

{

char str[] = "Rest in peace";   /* base address is 7004 */

char *ptr = &str[8];

printf ("%s", ptr++ +2);

return 0;

}
```

ANSWER: ace

Pointer **ptr** is assigned the address of 8th character of string **str[]** which is the address of character 'p' i, e **ptr** points to **(7012)**. The expression **ptr++ +2** yields the address of string **"ace"** which gets printed.

Q25. What will be the output of below C code?

```c
#include <stdio.h>

int main()
```

```c
{
char ch = 'A';

printf ("%d %d %d", sizeof(ch), sizeof('A'), sizeof(4.414));

return 0;

}
```

ANSWER: 1 4 8

Variable **ch** is of **char** type hence it will take 1 byte. Also, in C, a character constant is actually replaced by its ASCII value when stored in memory location which is of **int** type and **int** takes 4 bytes on 32-bit and 2 bytes on 16-bit system. A real number in C is **double** by default hence sizeof(4.414) will be 8 bytes.

Q26. What will be the output of below C code?

```c
#include <stdio.h>

int main()

{
char str[] = "North Carolina";

char arr[20];

char *ptr1 = str;

char *ptr2 = arr;

while (*ptr2++ = *ptr1++);

printf ("%s", arr);

return 0;

}
```

ANSWER: North Carolina

Here our program is copying each character of string **str[]** into a target string **arr[]**. Size of string **arr[]** should be enough sufficient to hold all characters of **str[]**. **ptr1** and **ptr2** are two **char** pointers which points to 0th memory location of array **str[]** and **arr[]** respectively. Through a while **loop** all characters of array **str[]** are being copied into **arr[]**, see how copying is done, this is a short way of implementing **strcpy** () function in C.

Q27. What will be the output of below C code?

```
#include <stdio.h>

int main()

{

char str[10];

int j;

for (j = 0; j <=8; j++)

*(str + j) = 65;

*(str + j) = '\0';

printf ("%s", str);

return 0;

}
```

ANSWER: AAAAAAAAA

Here, expression **(str + i)** will give the address of ith element from base address of string **str[]** and ***(str + i)** would give the character stored over there. Through the, **for** loop we stored character 'A' to those locations using ASCII value of 'A' which is 65. When **for** () loop terminates the value of **i** is 9 and at this index we store '\0' to mark the end of string.

Q28. What will be the output of below C code?

```c
#include <stdio.h>

int main()

{

char *ptr1 = "Hello C";

char *ptr2 = "Hello C++";

ptr1 = ptr2;

ptr2 = "Hello Java";

printf ("%s %s ", ptr1, ptr2);

return 0;

}
```

ANSWER: Hello C++ Hello Java

As we know that when a string is declared like this then we can easily change the pointers to point something else but the string can't be changed or modified anyhow. Initially, pointers **ptr1** and **ptr2** were pointing to "Hello C" and "Hello C++" respectively. Later on **ptr1** is assigned to **ptr2** hence now **ptr1** points to "Hello C++" and **ptr2** is assigned to a new string "Hello Java". These all operations are perfectly valid and finally **printf** () prints the expected output.

Q29. What will be the output of below C code?

```c
#include <stdio.h>

int main()

{

char str[] = "Learn C";
```

```c
char *ptr = "Learn Java";

str = "Learn C++";

ptr = "Learn Perl";

printf ("%s %s", str, ptr);

return 0;

}
```

ANSWER: Compilation error.

Clearly, we are initializing the **str** to a new string "Learn C++" which is not valid. You can change/modify the contents of **str** but you can't re-initialize the **str** to another new string. I have already discussed the issues regarding this type of case.

Q30. What will be the output of below C code?

```c
#include <stdio.h>

int main()

{

printf ("%u %s", &"Learn C", &"Learn Java");

return 0;

}
```

ANSWER: Base address of string "Learn C" and Learn Java

Note- **%u** gives address and **%s** uses this address to print the string.

Q31. What will be the output of below C code?

```c
#include<stdio.h>

int main()
```

```c
{
char arr[] = "Humpty Dumpty";

char *ptr1 = arr;

char *ptr2 = ptr1 + 3;

printf ("ptr2 - ptr1 = %d\n", ptr2 - ptr1);

printf ("(int*)ptr2 - (int*) ptr1 = %d",  (int*)ptr2 - (int*)ptr1);

return 0;

}
```

ANSWER: ptr2 - ptr1 = 3

               (int*)ptr2 - (int*) ptr1 = 0

Q32. What will be the output of below C code?

```c
#include <stdio.h>

int main()

{
const char *ptr = "Hello";

*ptr = 'W';

char *ptr1 = ptr;

ptr = "Bye";

printf ("%s %s", ptr1, ptr);

return 0;

}
```

ANSWER: Compilation error.

Here, string "Hello" is of **const** type and hence gets stored in read only location of "Data segment" of RAM. Any variable having **const** qualifier with it can't be changed. But pointer **ptr** is not of **const** type hence it gets stored in stack segment of RAM and it can point to some other memory locations.

Note:- Today many standard C compilers treat a C string as of **const** type implicitly. So there is no need of placing a **const** qualifier before a string. Any approach towards changing the string, will lead to segmentation fault.

Q33. What will be the output of below C code?

#include <stdio.h>

int main()

{

char const *ptr = "Hello";

*ptr = 'W';

char *ptr1 = ptr;

ptr = "Bye";

printf ("%s %s", ptr1, ptr);

return 0;

}

ANSWER: Compilation error.

Again string "Hello" is of **const** type. Rest of the explanations are same as that of Q32.

Q34. What will be the output of below C code?

#include <stdio.h>

int main()

```
{

char * const ptr = "Hello";

*ptr = 'W';

char *ptr1 = ptr;

ptr = "Bye";

printf ("%s %s", ptr1, ptr);

return 0;

}
```

ANSWER: Compilation error.

This time pointer **ptr** is **const** and is initially assigned to the base address of string "Hello". It can't point to some other memory location now. Here, **ptr** gets stored in read only section of "Data Segment" of RAM. Also, many compilers treat a C string as of **const** type and due to which you can't alter the given string "Hello" to "Wello", if it happens then it will lead to segmentation fault.

Q35. What will be the output of below C code?

```
#include <stdio.h>

int main()

{

const char * const ptr = "Hello";

*ptr = 'W';

char *ptr1 = ptr;

ptr = "Bye";

printf ("%s %s", ptr1, ptr);
```

return 0;

}

ANSWER: Compilation error.

Both, the pointer **ptr** as well as the string "Hello" are of **const** type.

Q36. What will be the output of below C code?

```c
#include <stdio.h>

const char *func()

{

return "Hello";

}

int main()

{

char *ptr = func(); /* Line 1 */

*ptr = 'W';        /* Line 2 */

printf ("%s", ptr);

return 0;

}
```

ANSWER: Compilation error at Line 1 and segmentation fault at Line 2.

The function **func** () returns a pointer to a constant string "Hello" but we are collecting that pointer in **non-const** pointer **ptr** inside **main** (). This incompatibility leads to compilation failure. Place **const** qualifier before **char *ptr** to compile the code successfully. But at run time, there will be segmentation fault because we can't alter a constant string. Old compilers like Turbo C don't give segmentation fault error, they treat a string as **non-const**. Many modern compilers will give segmentation fault at run time.

Q37. What is strlen () in C?

ANSWER: **strlen** () is a standard C library function defined in string.h header file and it returns the length of the string i, e the number of characters in the string excluding '\0' (null character).

Prototype declaration- **size_t strlen(char const *string)**;

Q38. What is strcmp () in C?

ANSWER: **strcmp** () is a standard C library function defined in string.h header file and it is used for lexicographic comparisons of two strings. It returns 0 if two string matches otherwise it returns the numeric difference between the ASCII values of the first non-matching pairs of characters.

Prototype declaration- **int strcmp(const char *str1, const char *str2)**;

Q39. What is strcpy () in C?

ANSWER: **strcpy** () is a standard C library function defined in string.h header file and it is used for copying one string to another string. If we call **strcpy(str1, str2)** then **strcpy** copies str2 into str1 including null character ('\0').

Prototype declaration- **char * strcpy(char *str1, const char *str2)**;

Here, **str1** is a pointer to destination string whereas **str2** is a pointer to source string and it returns a **char** pointer to destination string **str1**.

Q40. What will be the output of below C code?

#include <stdio.h>

#include <string.h>

int main()

```
{

char str[] = "Chandra\0Prakash";

printf ("%s %d %d", str, sizeof(str), strlen(str));

return 0;

}
```

ANSWER: Chandra 16 7

Since there is a null character ('\0') after 'a' of given string, hence **%s** prints the string "Chandra" only. Compiler finds a ('\0') after character 'a' so it thinks that the given string ends here. **sizeof(str)** gives 16 because all characters have occupied memory location of 1 byte each. **strlen(str)** gives the length of given string "Chandra" which is 7 because there is a ('\0') after character 'a' so **strlen** () just counts all character before first ('\0').

Q41. What is strcat () in C?

ANSWER: **strcat** () is a standard C library function defined in string.h and it is used to append a copy of a string at the end of another string.

Prototype declaration- **char *strcat(char *str1, const char *str2)**

Q42. What will be the output of below C code?

```
#include <stdio.h>

#include <string.h>

int main()

{

char *str1 = "Front";

char *str2 = "End";

char *ptr = strcat(str1, str2);
```

```
printf ("%s", ptr);

return 0;

}
```

ANSWER: Run time error (Program may crash as happened in my case).

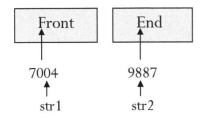

7004   9887

str1   str2

From above figure, it is clear that string **"Front"** is stored at memory location starting from 7004 (base address of 'F') whereas string **"End"** is stored at 9887 (base address of 'E'). Also, it is not known forehand that what is present in memory beyond **"Front"**. Pointers str1 and str2 are pointing to completely different locations as shown in the fig. hence it is unsafe to append the string **"End"** after the end of first one. Program may crash as it happened in my case.

Q43. Which C statement must be written to replace the code written at Line 1 to successfully run our program (i, e segmentation fault doesn't occur)?

```
#include <stdio.h>

void func(char *str1, char *str2)

{

int x = strlen(str1);

int y = strlen(str2);

int j;

for (j = 0; j <= y; j++)

str1[x + j] = str2[j];
```

```
}

int main()

{

char *str1 = "Back";   /* Line 1 */

char *str2 = "End";

func(str1, str2);

printf("%s", str1);

return 0;

}
```

ANSWER: char str1[20] = "Back";

Function **func** () is doing the same job what the **strcat** () does. But inside **main** () **char *str1** must be replaced by **char str1[20]**. Now it is completely safe to append the string **"End"** because we know that **str1** has now enough memory space to accommodate those characters of string **str2**.

Q44. What will be the output of below C code?

```
#include <stdio.h>

#include <string.h>

int main()

{

char str[20];

char *ptr = "GATE2004";

int length = strlen(ptr);

int i;
```

```c
for (i = 0; i < length; i++)

str[i] = ptr[length - i];

printf("%s",  str);

return 0;

}
```

ANSWER: Nothing will be printed on the console.

G	A	T	E	2	0	0	4	'\0'
7004	7005	7006	7007	7008	7009	7010	7011	7012

ptr

strlen () returns 8 and is assigned to variable **length**. Inside **for** loop, for i = 0, expression **str[i]** will be str[8 - 0] i, e **str[8]** which is '\0' located at 7012 location. See figure. Hence, '\0' gets stored at 0th index of **str[]** and **str[0]** contains '\0' as it's very first element. It doesn't matter what comes in after 0th index, compiler will neglect all characters and hence nothing gets printed.

Q45. What will be the output of below C code?

```c
#include <stdio.h>

int main()

{

char str[]  = "Concepts";

char *ptr  = str;

while (*ptr != '\0')

++*ptr++;

printf ("%s %s", str, ptr);
```

return 0;

}

ANSWER: Dpodfqut

Well, it's a funny output we are getting here. Basically, in this question we are changing each character of array **str[]**. The expression **++*ptr++** is actually doing everything. Here, firstly **++(*ptr)** will be executed by compiler hence ***ptr** yields 'C' which gets incremented by **++** (prefix operator) to become 'D' and then finally postfix **++** operator increments the pointer **ptr** to point to the next memory location i,e just next to the memory location where 'C' was stored.

Q46. What will be the output of below C code?

#include <stdio.h>

int main()

{

char str[]= "geeks\narecrazy";

char *ptr1, *ptr2;

ptr1 = &str[3];

ptr2 = str + 5;

printf ("%c", ++*str - --*ptr1 + *ptr2 + 2);

printf ("%s", str);

return 0;

}

ANSWER: heejs

        arecrazy

Here, initially pointers **ptr1** and **ptr2** are pointing to 'k' and '\n' respectively. Also, inside the **printf** (), the expression **++*str** increments the value stored at 0th index of **str[]** and **--*ptr1** decrements the value being pointed by **ptr1**. Hence, 'g' becomes 'h' and 'k' becomes 'j' due to these operations. So, final expression inside **printf** () will be-

printf ("%s", 'h' - 'j' + '\n' + 2) ➜ printf ("%s", -2 + '\n' + 2) and finally **'\n'** gets printed by **printf** ().

Note- ASCII ('h') - ASCII ('j') = -2

Q47. What will be the output of below C code?

```
#include <stdio.h>

void swap(char *str1, char *str2)

{

char *t = str1;

str1 = str2;

str2 = t;

}

int main()

{

char *str1 = "Hello";

char *str2 = "World";

swap (str1, str2);

printf ("str1 is %s and str2 is %s", str1, str2);

return 0;

}
```

ANSWER: str1 = "Hello" and str2 = "World"

Function **swap** () has been called just by passing the copies of the addresses of both strings as an argument. Inside **swap** (), we are just changing the local pointer variables and this effect is local (only for **swap** ()), not for **main** (). Hence, strings remain unchanged. If you want to swap the strings then pass the addresses as **"call by reference"** i, e send pointer to a pointer.

Q48. What will be the output of below C code?

```c
#include <stdio.h>

#include <string.h>

int main()

{

char *str[] = {"An", "apple", "a", "day", "keeps", "doctor", "away"};

printf ("%d %d %d", sizeof(str), sizeof(str[1]), strlen(str[0]));

return 0;

}
```

ANSWER: 28 4 2

An	apple	a	day	keeps	doctor	away
7004	9898	8076	7846	4765	100023	7682

str[]:

7004	9898	8076	7846	4765	100023	7682
6552	6556	6560	6564	6568	6572	6576

The given string **str[]** is nothing but an array of pointers to strings. From above figure, it's clear that elements of array **str[]** are pointers to strings, stored at some other memory locations. Hence, base address of "An" is stored in **str[0]**, base address of "apple" is stored in **str[1]** and so on. Go through the figure, things will be clear to you. There are total 7 addresses so total 7 * 4 i, e 28 bytes. 9898 is stored at **str[1]** so it will take 4 bytes of memory on 32-bit system and length of **str[1]** is 2.

Q49. What will be the output of below C code?

#include <stdio.h>

#include <string.h>

int main()

{

char str[6][50] = {

          "Somebody wants you, somebody needs you",
          "Somebody dreams about you every single night",
          "Somebody can't breathe, without you it's lonely",
          "Somebody hopes that one day you will see",
          "That somebody's me",
          "That somebody's me"

       };

printf ("%c %c", *(str[3] + 2), *(str[4] + strlen(str[4]) - 18));

return 0;

}

ANSWER: m T

Here **str** is a 2-D array which comprises of 1-D arrays, each of which is 50 characters long. We also that **str[i]** would give the base address of each of these 1-D arrays. **str[3]** would give the base address of 4th 1-D array say it is 65512. Hence, expression **(str[3] + 2)** will be equivalent to **(65512 + 2 * 1)** i, e **(65514)** and at this location 'm' is stored, ***(65514)**, which gets printed by %c. **strlen(str[4])** gives the length of the string stored at **str[4]** location. As you can see length is 18 hence expression ***(str[4] + strlen(str[4]) - 18)** is equivalent to ***(str[4] + 18 - 18)** i, e ***(str[4] + 0)** and at this memory location, 'T' is stored which gets printed.

Q50. What will be the output of below C code?

```c
#include <stdio.h>

int main()
{
char *str[] = { "Health", "is", "wealth"};

char **ptr = str;

printf("%s ", ++*ptr);

printf("%s ", *ptr++);

printf("%s ", ++*ptr);

return 0;

}
```

ANSWER: ealth ealth s

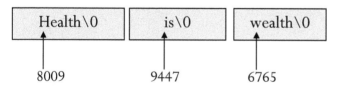

Health\0	is\0	wealth\0
8009	9447	6765

str[]:

8009	9447	6765
65512	65516	65520

ptr

The expression **++*ptr** has two operators of same precedence hence associativity comes into play. Firstly, expression **(*ptr)** will yield 8009, you know how? Then pre-increment **(++)** operator will increment the pointer to point 2nd character of "Health" which is '**e**' and hence **%s** prints the string "ealth". Similarly, for expression **(*ptr++),** we have two unary operators- ***** and **++** but **++** occurs after the **ptr**, so firstly ***(ptr)** is performed which yields **8010** (last time **ptr** was pointing to this location) but this value is not being assigned to any variable it gets ignored and hence **%s** again prints the string "ealth" and then pointer **ptr** will be incremented by 1 to point **65516** memory location. Last **printf** () prints "s" because the expression **++*ptr** will work as-

1. ***(ptr)** = ***(65516)** = **9447**

2. **++(9447)** = **9448** which is the address of "s".

Note: - Here **9447** is not rvalue but it is lvalue, address of character 's'. Hence on doing **++** it will increment the pointer so that memory location becomes **9448** from **9447**.

Q51. What will be the output of below C code?

```
#include <stdio.h>

char str[4][10] = {

                "Alaska",

                "Atlanta",

                "New York",

                "Seattle"

                };

int j;

char *temp;
```

```
temp = str[1];

str[1] = str[2];

str[2] = temp;

for (j = 0; j < 4; ++j)

printf ("%s", str[j]);

return 0;

}
```

ANSWER: Compilation error- "Lvalue required in main ()".

As we know **str[i]** contain the base address of each 1-D array of 2-D array. Actually, the statement **str[1] = str[2]** is erroneous because through this statement we are trying to interchange the base addresses stored in **str[1]** and **str[2]** which is not allowed in C. This is a very important concept in C which tells how the C compiler deals with string. Compilers keep track of any string by storing its base address. Hence, starting address of a string is not a "Lvalue" and can't be altered anyhow.

Q52. Will the following C program compile?

```
#include <stdio.h>

int main()

{

char *str;

scanf ("%s", str);   /* Enter any string but not a multi word string */

printf ("Entered string is %s", str);

return 0;
```

}

ANSWER: Compilation error.

We can't use scanf (), gets () and fgets () with an uninitialized pointer since it contains garbage value and does not point to any valid memory locations. It is not allowed in C.

Note: - If we are bound to do something like this then first allocate memory using **malloc** () and then pass this location in **scanf** () etc.

Your program will go like this-

char *ptr = (char *)malloc(10);

scanf ("%s", ptr);

Q53. What will be the output of below C code?

```c
#include <stdio.h>

#include <string.h>

#include <stdlib.h>

void func(char **ptr)

{

++ptr;

}

int main()

{

char *str = (char *)malloc (100 * sizeof(char));

strcpy(str, "Hello");
```

func(&str);

printf ("%s", str);

return 0;

}

ANSWER: Hello

At first sight most of us think that output will be "ello" but it is not so. If you see carefully then you will come to know that pointer **ptr** is local to the function **func** () and **++ptr** will increment this local pointer.

The figure is depicting every hidden concept. Clearly str, is containing the base address of string "Hello" and address of **str** i, e 8765 is passed to **func** (). Hence **ptr** would contain 8765 as shown in fig. When we do **++ptr** then actually we do **++** on **ptr**'s content i, e on 8765 but it is local for **func** () and hence effect gets localized for **func** () only. To actually print "ello", we will have to replace **++ptr** by **(*ptr)++**.

Q54. What will be the output of below C code?

#include <stdio.h>

int main()

{

char *str[] = {"Perl", "Lisp", "Ruby", "Java"};

char **strp[] = {str + 3, str + 2, str + 1, str};

```c
char ***strpp = strp;

printf ("%s", **++strpp);

printf ("%s", *--*++strpp+3);

printf ("%s", *strpp[-2]+3);

printf ("%s", strpp[-1][-1]+1);

return 0;

}
```

ANSWER: Ruby l a isp

The figure drawn below depicts everything. Before solving any question like this, you should first draw the memory arrangement diagram for better understanding of the problem. Go through the figure first, if you can draw at your own then go for it if you stuck somewhere, refer my figure for further steps.

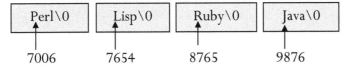

Perl\0	Lisp\0	Ruby\0	Java\0
7006	7654	8765	9876

str[]:

7006	7654	8765	9876
65512	65516	65520	65524

strp[]:

65524	65520	65516	65512
75512	75516	75520	75524

strpp

Clearly, pointer **strpp** contains **75512** hence expression ****++strpp** will first increment the **strpp** by 1 so that now **strpp** points to **75516** and then ****(75516)** may be treated as ***(*(75516))** which is equivalent to ***(6550)** and it gives base address of the string "Ruby" which gets printed.

Now in expression ***--*++strpp+3**, **strpp** is pointing to **75516**, **++(75516)** will give **75520** and ***(75520)** will give **(65516)**. Now on doing **--(65516)** will give **(65512)** and ***(65512)** will give base address of the string "Perl" i, e **7006** and finally **(7006 + 3 * 1)** will give **(7009)** which gets passed to **printf** () and **%s** prints the string starting from this location till '\0'. Clearly it will print "l\0".

Pointer **strpp** is currently pointing to **75520** and expression ***strpp[-2]+3** can be written as- ***(*(strpp - 2)) + 3** which is equivalent to ***(*(75520 - 2 * 4)) + 3** i, e ***(*(75512)) + 3** which is equivalent to ***(65524) + 3** and at ***(65524)** base address of string "Java" is stored i, e **9876** and adding 3 to this location will give **(9876 + 3 * 1)** i, e **(9879)** which gets passed to **printf** () and **%s** prints the string starting from **9879** to **9880** i,e "a\0".

Also, **strpp[-1][-1] + 1** can also be written as ***(*(strpp - 1) - 1) + 1**. Kindly do this at your own. Just do as we did in previous questions.

struct, union & enum

Q1. What will be the output of below C code?

```c
#include <stdio.h>

struct test
{
int data;
char ch;
float f;
};

void func1(struct test);

void func2(struct test *);

int main()
{
struct test t = {200, 'A', 35.23};

func1 (t);

func2 (&t);

return 0;
}

void func1(struct test t)
{
printf ("%d %c %f", t->data, t->ch, t->f);
```

}

void func2 (struct test *t)

{

printf ("%d %c %f", t.data, t.ch, t.f);

}

ANSWER: Compilation error.

The function **func1** () is collecting a structure variable in **t** and the **printf** () is trying to print the structure elements using arrow operator (->) with structure variable **t** which is an error in C because to access a structure element, on the left hand side of arrow operator (->), we must have a pointer to a structure not a structure variable. Similarly, **func2** () is collecting a structure pointer but **printf** () is trying to print the structure elements using dot operator (.) but the left hand side of a dot operator must be a structure variable not a structure pointer hence we get compile time error.

Q2. What will be the output of below C code?

#include <stdio.h>

#include <stdlib.h>

struct Node

{

int data;

struct node *next;

};

struct Node *ptr1, *ptr2;

ptr1 = (struct Node *)malloc(sizeof(struct Node));

```c
ptr2 = (struct Node *)malloc(sizeof(struct Node));
printf ("%d %d", sizeof(*ptr1), sizeof(*ptr2));
printf ("%d %d", sizeof(ptr1), sizeof(ptr2));
return 0;
}
```

ANSWER: 8 8 4 4   (On 32-bit system)

Pointers **ptr1** and **ptr2** are structure pointers hence they will take 4 bytes of memory space. **malloc** () is standard library function which allocates as many memory as its argument specifies. (***ptr1**) and (***ptr2**) are nothing but the size of the **struct Node**.

Q3. What will be the output of below C code?

```c
#include <stdio.h>
struct demo
{
int data;
struct demo link;
};
int main()
{
struct demo d;
d.data = 100;
d.link = d;
printf ("%d", d.link.data);
```

return 0;

}

ANSWER: Compile time error.

In C, structures are not allowed to contain a member of its own type because if this happens then it becomes impossible for compiler to know size of such structures.

Note: - A structure in C can contain a pointer of its type as its member because pointers of all types are of same size

---

Q4. What is wrong with the following C structure declaration?

#include <stdio.h>

struct Node

{

int data;

struct Node *next;

};

ANSWER: No error. This is a perfectly valid structure declaration. Such type of structure declaration is known as "Self referential" structure. As we know that a structure can contain a pointer of its type as its member hence in this declaration, **next** is a pointer of type **struct Node** and the compiler knows the size of **next** which is 4 bytes on 32-bit system. Hence there will be no problem of allocating memory for this structure by the compiler.

Q5. Compiler allocates memory for the members of a structure only when a structure variable is defined not when the structure is declared. [True/False]

ANSWER: True.

Q6. What will be the output of below C code?

```c
#include <stdio.h>

int main()

{

struct test

{

char str[] = "Concepts In C";

float price = 400.00;

};

struct test *ptr;

printf ("%s ", ptr - > str);

printf ("%f", ptr -> price);

return 0;

}
```

ANSWER: Compile time error.

As we know structures and unions are user defined data type i, e when we declare a structure or union, we actually declare a new data type of our need. We are not allowed to initialize values as it is not a variable declaration but a user defined data type declaration.

Q7. Can we have a nested structure in C? [Yes/No]

ANSWER: Yes.

Q8. What will be the output of below C code?

#include <stdio.h>

```c
int main()
{
struct Outer
{
int x;
char ch;
struct Inner
{
char c;
float f;
}inn;
};
struct Outer out = {100, 'A', 'a', 22.32};
printf ("%d %d %c %f", out.x, out.ch, out.inn.c, out.inn.f);
return 0;
}
```

ANSWER: 100 65 a 22.320000

Here we are doing nesting of structures i, e one structure is being declare within another structure. But it is necessary inner structure must declares structure variable otherwise we can't access the data member of inner structure. Accessing inner structure's member will go like this- **out.inn.f**.

Q9. What will be the output of below C code?

#include <stdio.h>

```
struct test

{

int x;

static int y;

};

int main()

{

struct test t;

printf ("%d", sizeof(t));

return 0;

}
```

ANSWER: Compile time error.

In C, structures and unions can't have static members.

Q10. What does the following structure declaration signify in C?

```
struct Node

{

int data;

float j;

}

struct Node *s[10];
```

ANSWER: **s** is an array of 10 pointers to a structure of type Node.

Q11. What will be the output of below C code?

```c
#include <stdio.h>
#include <string.h>
struct demo
{
char str[20];
};
int main()
{
struct demo q;
strcpy (q.str, "Hello C");
printf ("%s", q.str);
return 0;
}
```

ANSWER: Hello C

Q12. What will be the output of below C code?

```c
#include <stdio.h>
struct info
{
char str[20];
int age;
float sal;
};
```

```c
int main()
{
struct info i;
i.str = "Jack";
i.age = 20;
printf ("%s %d", i.str, i.age);
return 0;
}
```

ANSWER: Compile time error- "Lvalue required"

The statement- **i.str = "Jack"** is erroneous because **str** is not a l-value because we know that a modifiable l-value cannot have an array type, an incomplete type, or a type with the **const** attribute. Hence it results into compilation failure.

Q13. What will be the output of below C code?

```c
#include <stdio.h>

#include <string.h>

struct city
{
char *name;

int pin_code;

};
int main()
{
{
```

struct city ct1 = {"Dublin", 1194};

struct city ct2 = ct1;

strupr (ct2.name);

printf ("%s", ct1.name);

return 0;

}

ANSWER: Run time exception

In C, the values of a structure variable can be assigned to another structure variable of the same type using assignment operator (=). Always remember, it is only the assignment operator (=) that can be applied on a structure variable. *No other operators can work on structure variables.*

Here all elements of structure variable **ct1** have been assigned to **ct2** which is not an error but using **strupr** () to convert a constant string to uppercase causes a run time exception. Constant strings can't be altered.

Note: - To successfully run this program, we should have following structure declaration-

struct city

{

char name[20];

int pin_code;

};

The strings created using an array **[]** are modifiable as you must have studied in Chapter 8.

Q14. What will be the output of below C code?

#include <stdio.h>

```
struct city

{

char name[20];

int pin_code;

};

int main()

{

struct city ct1 = {"Auckland", 112};

struct city ct2 = ct1;

if (ct1 == ct2)

printf ("Both are equal");

else

printf ("Both are not equal");

return 0;

}
```

ANSWER: Compile time error- "no match for 'operator=='in 'ct1 == ct2'.

Structure variables can't be compared using == or != operators.

Q15. What will be the output of below C code?

```
#include <stdio.h>

struct city

{

char name[20];
```

```
char *str;

};

int main()

{

struct city ct = {"Sydney", "Ontario"};

printf ("%c %s ", ct.name[2], ct.str);

printf ("%s %c", ct.name, *((ct.name)+5));

return 0;

}
```

ANSWER: d Ontario Sydney y

Here "Sydney" gets stored in the array **name []** and "Ontario" gets stored starting from the memory location pointed by pointer **str**. In first **printf ()**, **name[2]** refers to the character stored at 2nd index of string "Sydney". Also, **str** points to string "Ontario" and to access these strings, we must use dot operator preceded by structure variable. You better know how to access a structure member using dot operator and structure variable. The expression **ct.name** yields the base address of string "Sydney". On adding 5 to this base address, we get the address of character '**y**' and dereferencing this address will give the character stored at that location which is nothing but '**y**'.

Q16. What will be the output of below C code?

```
#include <stdio.h>

struct city

{

char name[10];

int pin;
```

```
};

int main()

{

struct city ct[] = {

                {"Zurich", 132},

                {"Phoenix", 879},

                {"Amsterdam", 657}

        };

printf ("%d %s ", ct[0].pin, ct[2].name);

printf ("%s", (*(ct + 1)).name);

return 0;

}
```

ANSWER: 132 Amsterdam Phoenix

Here, **ct** is an array of structures of the type **struct city**.

ct[0].name	ct[0].pin	ct[1].name	ct[1].pin	ct[2].name	ct[1].pin
Zurich	132	Phoenix	879	Amsterdam	657
7000	7010	7014	7024	7028	7038

The figure is depicting, how array of structures are stored in memory. In an array of structures, all elements of the array are stored in adjacent memory locations. Hence, in the first **printf** (), **ct[0].pin** is nothing but 132 as shown in figure. Similarly, **ct[2].name** contains the base address of string "Amsterdam" which is used by **%s** to print this string. In the last **printf** (), **ct** is a pointer, you know why? and hence on adding **1** to it, we will get the base address of the structure starting from **7014** memory location and ***(ct + 1)** is nothing but **ct[1]** and hence **ct[1].name** will yield "Phoenix".

Q17. What will be the output of below C code?

```
#include <stdio.h>
#include <string.h>
struct test
{
char *str;
int j;
};
int main()
{
struct test t;
strcpy (t.str, "Hello C");
printf ("%s", t.str);
return 0;
}
```

ANSWER: Run Time Error.

Pointer **str** is uninitialized and hence it holds garbage value (address) and we have assigned the base address of the string "Hello World" to it. The result will be undefined because no one knows where the "Hello World" would have stored in memory.

Q18. What is the difference between structure and union in C?

ANSWER: The two main differences are as follows-

1. The memory occupied by structure variable is the sum of sizes of all the members but memory occupied by union variable is equal to space hold by the largest data member of a union.

2. In the structure, all the members are accessed at any point of time but in union only one of union member can be accessed at any given time.

Q19. Consider the following C declaration

struct

{

short s[5]

union

{

float y;

long z;

}u;

} t;

Assume that objects of the type **short, float** and **long** occupy 2 bytes, 4 bytes and 8 bytes, respectively. What will be the memory requirement for structure variable **t**?

ANSWER: **short** array s[5] will take 10 bytes as size of short is 2 bytes. When we declare a union, memory allocated for the union is equal to memory needed for the largest member of it, and all members share this same memory space. Since **u** is a union, memory allocated to u will be max of **float** y(4 bytes) and **long** z(8 bytes). So, total size will be 18 bytes (10 + 8).

Q20. What will be the output of below C code? Assume that the size of an integer is 4 bytes and size of character is 1 byte. Also assume that there is no alignment needed.

```
#include <stdio.h>

union test

{

int i;

char str[10];

float j;

};

int main()

{

printf ("%d", sizeof(union test));

return 0;

}
```

ANSWER: 10

When we declare a union, memory allocated for a union variable of the type is equal to memory needed for the largest member of it, and all members share this same memory space. In above example, **char str[10]** is the largest member. Therefore size of **union test** is 10 bytes.

Q21. What will be the output of below C code on a 16-bit compiler?

```
#include <stdio.h>

int main()

{

union u

{
```

int x;

char ch[2];

}key;

key.ch[0] = 0;

key.ch[1] = 2;

key.ch[1] = 0;

key.ch[1] = 0;

printf ("%d", key.x);

return 0;

}

ANSWER: 512

Let's go through the representation of this data type in memory of a little-endian architecture for better understanding-

←					key.x							→
Low Bytes are stored here							High Bytes are stored here					
←			key.ch[0]			→	←			key.ch[1]		→

0	0	0	0	0	0	1	0	0	0	0	0	0	0	0	0

Clearly, this is how 512 will be stored in memory.

Q22. What will be the output of below C code?

#include <stdio.h>

int main()

```
{
union u
{
int x, y;
}key;
key.x = 2;
key.y = 4;
printf ("%d", key.x);
return 0;
}
```

ANSWER: 4

Always remember that we can't assign different values to the different union elements at the same time. Whenever we assign a value to any union member then it gets automatically assigned to other union members as well.

Q23. What will be the output of below C code?

```
#include <stdio.h>
union test
{
int i;
char str[4];
};
int main()
{
```

```c
union test t;

t.i = 0;

t.str[1] = 'C';

printf ("%s", t.str);

return 0;

}
```

ANSWER: Nothing will be printed on the console.

As we know, **i** and **str[4]** will share the same memory space hence when we do **t.i = 0** then all spaces of **str[]** also gets set to 0 and the character corresponding to this ASCII value is '**\0**' which occupies all spaces of array **str[]**. Now after, **t.str[1] = 'C'**, our array **str[]** is like- "\0C\0\0..." and since '**\0**' is placed at 0th index hence **%s** will print nothing because '\0' is mark of the end of a string in C.

Q24. What is wrong with following C code?

```c
#include <stdio.h>

int main()

{

union u;

{

int x;

char str[2];

};

union u a1 = {128};

union u a2 = {0, 4};
```

return 0;

}

ANSWER: In C, we can't initialize the other union members except the first member as we have done in this question. The C standard doesn't allow us to initialize the 2nd member like **union u a2 = {0, 4}** and which causes the compilation error.

Q25. What will be the output of below C code?

#include <stdio.h>

int main()

{

enum city {Mumbai, Dublin, Phoenix};

enum city ct1, ct2, ct3;

ct3 = Phoenix;

ct1 = Dublin;

ct2 = Mumbai;

printf ("%d %d %d", ct1, ct2, ct3);

return 0;

}

ANSWER: 1 0 2

Internally, the compilers treat the enumerators as integers. Each value of the enumerators corresponds to an integers starting with 0. Hence, **ct1** is stored as 0, **ct2** is stored as 1 and **ct3** is stored as 2.

Q26. What will be the output of below C code?

#include <stdio.h>

```c
int main()

{

enum lang {Java = -2, Ruby = 0, Perl, Lisp};

printf ("%d %d %d %d", ++Java, Ruby, Perl, Lisp};

return 0;

}
```

ANSWER: Compilation error.

Operators like ++ or -- do not work on enum values. These values are implicitly constant.

Note: - The enumerators can be assigned to different integer values by programmers. In above question, Perl is stored as 1 and Lips is stored as 2 and Java is stored as -2 and Ruby as 0.

Java + Ruby would give -2, this is acceptable but ++Java or --Java is not.

Q27. What will be the output of below C code?

```c
#include <stdio.h>

int main()

{

enum color {RED, PINK, BLUE, WHITE};

enum movie {RED, DHOOM, HEAT};

int i = 0;

for (i = RED; i <= WHITE; i++)

printf ("%d ", i);

 return 0;
```

}

ANSWER: Compile time error.

An enumeration constant must be unique within the scope in which it is defined and since enumeration constant **RED** appears two times in **main** () which is not allowed. If this happens, it will give compilation error.

Q28. What will be the output of below C code?

```c
#include <stdio.h>

struct test

{

int a;

char ch;

float s;

};

int main()

{

struct test t;

printf ("%u %u %u", &t.a, &t.ch, &t.s);

return 0;

}
```

ANSWER: 65518 65520 65521 (On TC/TC++)

2686768 2686772 2686776 (On 32-bit compilers)

First output is as expected, in memory **char** will be stored immediately after the **int** and **float** begins immediately after the **char**. But second output turns out to be different when run on today's modern 32-bit compilers like VC++

and Ideone, codepad etc. As you can observe that **float** doesn't get stored immediately after the **char**. There is a hole of 3 bytes after the **char**. This is called "Structure Padding" in C where a compiler may leave holes between data members to improve efficiency. Any 32-bit compilers are designed to generate the code for 32-bit processor and such processors are designed to fetch that data present at an address, which is a multiple of 4, much faster than the data present at any address.

Q29. How can we control the alignment of structure elements manually?

ANSWER: Many compilers provide a directive known as- **#pragma pack**. This directive specifies packing alignment for structure elements. Turbo C/C++ compiler doesn't support this feature but modern compilers like **VC++, Ideone and codepad** does.

For example-

```
#pragma pack(1)

#include <stdio.h>

struct test

{

int a;

char ch;

float s;

};

int main()

{

struct test t;

printf ("%u %u %u", &t.a, &t.ch, &t.s);
```

return 0;

}

ANSWER: 2686768 2686772 2686773 (On 32-bit compilers)

Did you see? The **float** gets stored immediately after the **char** in this case. Here, **#pragma pack(1)** lets each structure elements to be aligned at addresses which are multiple of 1.

Q30. What will be the output of below C code?

#include <stdio.h>

struct test

{

char ch;

int x;

long int y;

};

int main()

{

printf ("%d", sizeof(struct test));

return 0;

}

ANSWER: 12

Actually total size of this structure will be-

sizeof(char) + 3 bytes padding + sizeof(int) + sizeof(long int) = 1+3+4+4 = 12

There will be a padding of 3 bytes between **char** and **int**. You can check it by printing their addresses.

Q31. What will be the output of below C code?

```
#include <stdio.h>

struct test

{

short int i;

char ch;

int j;

};

int main()

{

struct test t;

printf ("%u %u %u ", &t.i, &t.ch, &t.j);

printf ("%d", sizeof(struct test));

return 0;

}
```

ANSWER: 2686784 2686786 2686788 8

The first member of **struct test** is **short int** followed by **char**. Since **char** can be on any byte boundary no padding required in between **short int** and **char** and it is also clear from the output. As you can see from the output **char** is immediately stored after **short int**. Hence they occupy 3 bytes. The next member is **int**. If the **int** is allocated immediately, it will start at an odd byte boundary which will not be a multiple of 4 (size of **int**). We need 1 byte padding after the **char** member to make the address of next **int** member is 4 byte aligned which is **2686788**, a multiple of 4. Hence total bytes allocated will be-

sizeof(short int) + sizeof(char) + (1 byte padding) + sizeof(int)

i, e (2 + 1 + 1 + 4) = 8 bytes.

Q32. What will be the output of below C code?

#include <stdio.h>

struct test

{

char ch;

double d;

int i;

};

int main()

{

printf ("%d", sizeof(struct test));

return 0;

}

ANSWER: 24

The output should be 20 or 24. Confusing, but the final answer is 24. Yes, but how? We know that here total size will be-

sizeof(char) + (7 bytes padding) + sizeof(double) + sizeof(int)

1 + 7 + 8 + 4 = 20. Still we are getting 24 bytes. I am leaving this question upto you to discover the reason behind it.

Q33. What will be the output of below C code?

```c
#include <stdio.h>
struct test
{
double d;
int i;
char ch;
}t;
int main()
{
printf ("%u %u %u ", &t.d, &t.i, &t.ch);
printf ("%d", sizeof(struct test));
return 0;
}
```

ANSWER: 4210704 4210712 4210716 16

It is clear from first three outputs that in this question no padding has been done by the compiler. By now, it may be clear that padding is unavoidable. There is a way to minimize padding. The programmer should declare the structure members in their increasing/decreasing order of size as we have done in this question since **sizeof(double) > sizeof(int) > sizeof(char)**.

Q34. What will be the output of below C code?

```c
#include <stdio.h>
int main()
{
```

```
struct city

{

char *str;

int pin;

struct city *ptr;

};

struct city arr[] = {

                {"Norway", 121, arr + 1},

                {"Phoenix", 232, arr + 2},

                {"Georgia", 876, arr}

        };

struct city *q = arr;

printf ("%s %s %s", arr[2].str, q[1].str, q[2].ptr->str);

return 0;

}
```

ANSWER: Georgia Phoenix Norway

Norway	Phoenix	Georgia

arr[0].str	arr[0].pin	arr[0].ptr	arr[1].str	arr[1].pin	arr[1].ptr	arr[2].str	arr[2].pin	arr[2].ptr
6537	121	1008	8341	232	1014	9087	876	1002
1002	1004	1006	1008	1010	1012	1014	1016	1018

q

| 1002 |

Structure **city** contains two pointers namely str and **ptr**, where **str** is of **char** type and **ptr** is a pointer to a structure. Pointer **ptr** stores the starting address of a structure variable of type **struct city**. Also, an array of structure **arr[]** has been declared as well as initialized. Now go through the figure, you will come to know that **arr[0].str** contains the base address of "Norway", **arr[0].pin** contains the integer value and **arr[0].ptr** contains the address of next structure variable. Same thing happens for other array elements. Clearly, **arr[2].str** contains base address of "Georgia" which gets printed by **%s**. Pointer **q** also points to base address of array **arr[]** hence **q[1].str** is same as **arr[1].str** which contains base address of "Phoenix" which also gets printed by **%s**. Now **q[2].ptr** is equivalent to arr[2].ptr which yields **1002**, base address of array **arr[]** and at this location base address of string "Norway" and to access it we will have to arrow operator (**->**) to print "Norway" by **%s**.

Q35. What will be the output of below C code?

```c
#include <stdio.h>

int main()

{

struct city

{

char *str;

struct city *ptr;

};

static struct city arr[] = {
                    {"Edinburg", arr + 2},
                    {"Dublin", arr},
                    {"Alaska", arr + 1}
```

```
                        };

struct city *q[3];

int j;

for (j = 0; j <= 2; ++j)

q[j] = arr[j].ptr;

printf ("%s %s %s", q[0]->str, (*q)->str, (**q));

return 0;

}
```

ANSWER: Alaska Alaska Alaska

q is an array of 3 three structure pointers i, e each element of array **q[]** will hold the address of a structure of the type **struct city**. This question resembles with Q34. Try this at your own. Draw figure first and then proceed as we did in previous question.

Q36. What do you mean by Object copy in C?

ANSWER: An object copy is an action in computing where a data object has its attributes copied to another object of the same data type as we do in assigning one structure variable to another structure variable of same type.

Q37. What do you mean by Shallow copy?

ANSWER: Let's consider two objects namely A and B.

This is one of the methods of copying an object. In the process of shallow copying A, B will copy all of A's field values. If the field value is a memory address it copies the memory address, and if the field value is a primitive type it copies the value of the primitive type. This method has a disadvantage- "if you modify the memory address that one of B's fields point to, you are also modifying what A's fields point to".

Q38. What do you mean by Deep copy?

ANSWER: This is an alternative method where the data is actually copied over. The result is different from the result a shallow copy gives. The advantage is that A and B do not depend on each other but at the cost of a slower and more expensive copy.

Q39. What will be the output of below C code?

```c
#include <stdio.h>
#include <string.h>
#include <stdlib.h>
struct city
{
char *str;
};
int main()
{
struct city ct1, ct2;
ct1.str = (char *)malloc(sizeof(20));
strcpy (ct1.str, "Edinburg");
ct2 = ct1;
ct1.str[0] = 'U';
ct1.str[1] = 'A';
printf ("ct1's str is: %s\n", ct1.str);
printf ("ct2's str is: %s\n", ct2.str);
```

return 0;

}

ANSWER: ct1's str is: UAinburg

ct2's str is: UAinburg

In C, when we assign a structure variable to another, all members of the variable are copied to the other structure variable. But what happens when the structure contains pointer to dynamically allocated memory as in this question. Here structure variable **ct1** contains pointer to dynamically allocated memory. When we assign, **ct1** to **ct2**, **str** pointer of **ct2** also start pointing to same memory location. This kind of copying is called Shallow Copy. The last two **printf** () has also printed the same string which clearly signifies that there is shallow copy in this program.

There may be a case where we have an array instead of dynamically allocated memory. Will there be Shallow copy or Deep copy? Let's check it out in our next question which deals with Deep copy.

Q40. What will be the output of below C code?

```
#include <stdio.h>
#include <string.h>
struct city
{
char str[20];
};
int main()
{
struct city ct1, ct2;
```

strcpy (ct1.str, "London");

ct2 = ct1;

ct1.str[0] = 'M';

printf ("ct1's string is: %s\n", ct1.str);

printf ("ct2's string is: %s\n", ct2.str);

return 0;

}

ANSWER: ct1's string is: Mondon

        ct2's string is: London

When we have an array instead of a dynamically allocated memory then always remember that we don't have shallow copy but compiler automatically performs Deep Copy for array members. In this question, structure **city** contains an array member **str[]**. When we assign **ct1** to **ct2**, **ct2** has a new copy of the array **str[]**. So **ct2** is not changed when we change **str[]** of **ct1**.

Chapter-10

File Operation In C

Q1. What will be the output of below C code?

```c
#include <stdio.h>

int main()

{

/* suppose input for this program is "Java" */

char str[20];

printf ("%d", scanf("%s", str));

return 0;

}
```

ANSWER: 1

scanf () always return the number of inputs it has successfully read.

Q2. What is EOF in C?

ANSWER: **EOF** is a macro constant defined as **#define EOF -1** in **stdio.h** header file which indicates the end of a C file. **EOF** is an integer value hence must always be assigned to an integer variable only.

Q3. What will be the output of below C code?

```c
#include <stdio.h>

int main()

{

unsigned char ch;
```

```c
FILE *fp;

fp = fopen ("file1.txt", "r");

while ((ch = getc(fp)) != EOF)

printf ("%c", ch);

fclose (fp);

return 0;

}
```

ANSWER: Run Time Error.

Here **getc** () is a macro not a function which reads the character from the current position (to which **fp** points) and advances the pointer position. The macro reads a single character and on success it returns the character (promoted to an **int** value). On the end of file or error it returns **EOF**. Here variable **ch** is of **unsigned char** type whose range is from 0 - 255 hence when **EOF** is returned by **getc** (), it can't be stored in **ch**.

Note: - **getc** () is also treated as a function in some libraries and a macro in some other libraries.

To successfully run this code, variable **ch** must be of **int** type.

Q4. What will be the output of below C code?

```c
#include <stdio.h>

int main()

{

FILE *ptr;

char ch;

ptr = fopen ("file1.txt", "r");
```

```
while ((ch = fgetc(ptr)) != NULL)

printf ("%c", ch);

return 0;

}
```

ANSWER: The program will generate an infinite loop.

NULL is defined as **#define NULL 0** whereas **EOF** is defined as **#define EOF -1**. The function **fgetc** () is similar to **getc** () which returns **EOF** when the end of a file is encountered. But we are checking the condition for **NULL** instead of **EOF** in the **while** loop which causes the the program to go into a infinite loop.

Q5. What will be the output of below C code?

```
#include <stdio.h>

int main()

{

// suppose file1.txt contains- Let's learn C

                //    And then C++

FILE *fp;

char ch;

int count = 1;

fp = fopen ("file1.txt", "r");

while ((ch = fgetc(fp)) != EOF))

{

if (ch == '\n')

++count;
```

```
}
```

printf ("%d", count);

fclose(fp);

return 0;

```
}
```

ANSWER: 2

The program simply counts the number of lines in the given file.

Q6. What will be the output of below C code?

#include <stdio.h>

int main()

```
{
```

printf("\nCOBOL\by");

printf("\rConcepts In C");

return 0;

```
}
```

ANSWER: "\n" followed by Concepts In C

The program first print a new line ("\n") and then COBOL but it gets erased by \b . Second printf has \r in it so it goes back to start of the line and starts printing characters.

Q7. What will be the output of below C code?

#include<stdio.h>

#include<string.h>

int main()

```
{
char str[100];

char str1[10], str2[10];

int i=0, max=0, len;

/* input a small paragraph */

gets(str);

 char *ptr = str;

while (*ptr)

{

if((*ptr!=' ') && (*ptr!='.') && (*ptr!=','))

str1[i] = *ptr;

else

str1[i] = '\0';

if(*ptr == ' '|| *ptr == '.'|| *ptr == ',')

{

len = strlen(str1);

if (len > max)

{

max = len;

strcpy (str2, str1);

}

}
```

```c
if ((*ptr == ' ')||(*ptr == '.')||(*ptr == ','))

i=0;

else

i++;

ptr++;

}
printf("\n");

printf("Longest string is: %s and its length is: %d\n",str2,max);

return 0;

}
```

ANSWER: The program will print the longest string in a given paragraph and also the length of that longest string.

Note: - The program only consider full stop (.), comma (,) and space(' ') in the given paragraph. You may also include other punctuations as well.

Q8. What is fseek () in C?

ANSWER: **fseek** () is a function defined in **stdio.h** header file which moves the file pointer from one record to another. Prototype declaration of **fseek** () is-

int fseek(FILE *fp, long displacement, int origin);

fp is a file pointer, **displacement** is a **long** integer which can be positive or negative and it denotes the number of bytes the pointer should be moved from a particular position. The last argument **origin** is the position relative to which the displacement takes place.

Q9. What do you mean by following function calls in C?

1. fseek (fp, -disp, SEEK_CUR);

2. fseek (fp, 0, SEEK_END);

3. fseek (fp, +disp, SEEK_SET);

ANSWER: In the first function call, **-disp** moves the file pointer back by **disp** bytes from the current position. **SEEK_CUR** is a macro defined in **stdio.h** header file.

In the second function call, 0 or (**+/- disp**) are in fact **offset** that tell the compiler by how many bytes should the pointer be moved from a particular position. **SEEK_END** is a macro which moves the pointer from the end of a file. **SEEK_SET** means move the pointer with reference to the beginning of the file.

Q10. What will be the output of below C code?

```c
#include <stdio.h>

int main()

{

/* file contains "We are in Edinburg" */

FILE *fp;

char ch, str[10];

fp = fopen ("file.txt", "r");

fseek (fp, 10L, SEEK_CUR);

fgets (str, 8, fp);

puts (str);

return 0;

}
```

Q11. What will be the output of below C code?

#include <stdio.h>

int main()

{

/* file contains "We are in Edinburg" */

FILE *fp;

char str[15];

fp = fopen ("file1.txt", "r");

fseek (fp, 10, SEEK_SET);

fgets (str, 8, fp);

fclose (fp);

return 0;

}

ANSWER: Compile time error.

fseek () need a long offset value. Don't pass **int**.

Chapter-11

Command Line Argument

Q1. What are the two arguments that we pass on to **main** () at command prompt?

ANSWER: The two arguments are- **argc** and **argv**.

Q2. What are argc and argv in C?

ANSWER: **argv** is an array of pointers to strings and **argc** is an **int** whose value is equal to the numbers of strings to which **argv** points.

Q3. What is the correct way of declaring main () when it receives arguments at command prompt?

ANSWER: **int main (int argc, char *argv[])**

Q4. Is it necessary to use argc and argv only for command line arguments?

ANSWER: No, we can use any valid identifiers in C instead of using **argc** and **argv**.

Q5. What will be the output of below C code when executed at command line? File name of the program is file1.c

file1

#include <stdio.h>

int main (int argc, char *argv[])

{

printf ("%s", argv[argc - 1]);

return 0;

}

ANSWER: On 32-bit compilers, we will get complete path of the file name-
"file1.exe".   This   is   what   I   got   on   my   system-
C:\Users\hp\Documents\file1.exe

Q6. Is it true that the 0th element of the argv array always contain the name of
the executable file?

ANSWER: True. **argv[0]** always contains the name of the executable file.

Q7. What will be the output of below C code when executed at command
line? File name of the program is file2.c

file2 11 22 33

#include <stdio.h>

int main (int argc, char *argv[])

{

int j;

for (j = 0; j < argc; ++j)

printf ("%s", argv[j]);

return 0;

}

ANSWER: C:\Users\hp\Documents\file2.exe 11 22 33

The path name may vary for your system.

argc would contain 4

argv[0] would contain base address of the string "file2".

argv[1] would contain base address of the string "11".

argv[2] would contain base address of the string "22".

argv[3] would contain base address of the string "33".

Q8. What will be the output of below C code when executed at command line? File name of the program is file3.c

file3

```
#include <stdio.h>

int main (int argc, char *argv[])

{

printf ("%d", argv[argc] + 3);

return 0;

}
```

ANSWER: 3

argc contains 1 because only one argument has been supplied and that is file3

argv[0] contains base address of the string "file3".

argv[1], argv[2],.......would contain 0 hence **argv[1] + 3** evaluates to 3.

Q9. What will be the output of below C code when executed at command line? File name of the program is file4.c

file4 11 22 33

```
#include <stdio.h>

#include <stdlib.h>

int main (int argc, char *argv[])

{

int m, n = 0;

for (m = 1; m < argc; ++m)
```

```
{
n += atoi (argv[m]);

printf ("%d", n);

return 0;

}
```

ANSWER: 66

In this program, we are calculating the sum of the elements of **argv[1]**, **argv[2]** and **argv[3]**. Since, these elements are not of **int** type but are strings hence we can't add them directly using + operator. **atoi** is a standard library function in C which is used to convert a string into an integer type. This function is defined in **stdlib.h** header file. Inside **for** () loop we are accessing each element of **argv[]** and converting each string into its integer equivalent by using **atoi** () and summing all integers values which comes out to be 66.

Note: - Don't use **atoi** () on **argv[0]** because it contains the base address of the string "file4" and **atoi** () can't convert a file name into its integer equivalent.

Q10. What will be the output of below C code when executed at command line? File name of the program is file5.c

file5 Java Lisp perl

```
#include <stdio.h>

int main (int argc, char *argv[])

{
char *ptr = 1[argv];

printf ("%s", ptr);

return 0;
```

}

ANSWER: Java

Here, **argv[1]** contains base address of the string "Java" which has been assigned to pointer **ptr**.

Q11. What will be the output of below C code when executed at command line? File name of the program is file6.c

file6 Java Lisp perl

#include <stdio.h>

int main (int argc, char *argv[])

{

++argv;

printf ("%s", *++argv);

return 0;

}

ANSWER: Lisp

Q12. Is it necessary to recompile the program every time we supply a new set of values to the program at command prompt?

ANSWER: No. We don't need to recompile every time.

Q13. Is it true that arguments supplied to the program at command prompt treated as strings?

ANSWER: Yes. Even if, you have supplied int/float as arguments at command prompt, they are treated as strings.

Q14. What will be the output of below C code when executed at command line? File name of the program is file7.c

file7 24.34 45.60 32.32

```c
#include <stdio.h>
#include <stdlib.h>
int main(int argc, char *argv[])
{
int j;
float fl = 0.0;
for (j = 1; j < argc; ++j)
fl += atof (argv[j]);
printf ("%f", fl);
return 0;
}
```

ANSWER: 102.259995

atof () is a standard library function defined in stdlib.h header file which is used to convert a string into its float equivalent.

Q15. What will be the output of below C code when executed at command line? File name of the program is file8.c

file8 Java Lisp perl

```c
#include <stdio.h>
int main (int argc, char *argv[])
{
```

printf ("%c", **++argv);

return 0;

}

ANSWER: J

Q16. What will be the output of below C code when executed at command line? File name of the program is file9.c

file9 Mon Wed Fri

```
#include <stdio.h>
int main (int argc, char *argv[])
{
int j;
for (j = 1; j < argc; ++j)
printf ("%c", *argv[j]);
return 0;
}
```

ANSWER: M W F

As we know **argv[j]** contain base address of each strings supplied at command prompt. Hence, **argv[1]** gives base address of string "Mon" and ***argv[1]** will give 'M' which gets printed by **%c**. Same concept applies for every member of **argv[]**. Actually we are not solving new types of questions but what we have learnt in Chapter 8, the same concept works here as well.

Q17. What will be the output of below C code when executed at command line? File name of the program is file10.c

file10 Hello world

```
#include <stdio.h>

int main (int argc, char *argv[])

{

printf ("%d %c", argc, (*++argv)[0]);

return 0;

}
```

ANSWER: 3 H

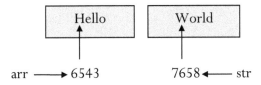

argv[]:

Base address of file10	6543	7658
65512	65516	65520

If you go through the figure, then you will come to know that the expression **(*++argv)[0]** is equivalent to **arr[0]** where arr is equal to **6543**. It is so because **++argv** gives **65516** and ***(65516)** gives **6543** which is base address of string "Hello" and from the figure, it is clear that **arr** points to **6543**. Hence, **%c** prints the character 'H'. Also, argc gives 3 because three arguments have been supplied at command prompt.

Q18. What will be the output of below C code when executed at command line? File name of the program is file11.c

file11 Ruby SmallTalk .NET JSP

```
#include <stdio.h>

int main (int argc, char *argv[])

{
```

```
while (argc--)

printf ("%s ", argv[argc]);

return 0;

}
```

ANSWER: JSP .NET SmallTalk Ruby file11

Try to figure out this question at your own.

Q19. What will be the output of below C code when executed at command line? File name of the program is file12.c

file12 Ajax jQuery xml

```
#include <stdio.h>

#include <string.h>

int main (int argc, char *argv[])

{

int len = strlen (argv[1]);

while (len-- > 0)

printf ("%c", argv[1][len]);

return 0;

}
```

ANSWER: lreP

Q20. What will be the output of below C code when executed at command line? File name of the program is file13.c

file13 Let's learn C

file 13 Let's learn C++

file 13 Let's learn Java

```c
#include <stdio.h>

int main (int argc, char *argv[])

{

printf ("%s", argv[0]);

return 0;

}
```

ANSWER: C:\Users\hp\Documents\file13.exe

The program will always output the same path name. You may get a different path name depending on your system setting. It will be independent of the number of arguments supplied at command prompt.

Chapter-12

Variadic Functions In C

Q1. Write prototype declaration of a standard library function in C which takes variable number of arguments.

ANSWER: int printf (const char *format, ...);

Q2. Which standard library function helps us in passing variable number of arguments to a function in C?

ANSWER: **stdarg.h**

Q3. What are **va_start**, **va_arg** and **va_list** in C?

ANSWER: These are three macros available in **stdlib.h** header file. These macros help in accessing the arguments of the function when the function takes a fixed number of arguments followed by variable number of arguments.

va_start macro initializes a pointer to the beginning of the list of optional arguments.

va_arg macro extracts an argument from the variable argument list and then advances the pointer to the next variable argument.

va_list macro is an array that holds information needed by **va_arg** and **va_end** and also used to declare the pointer of type **va_list**.

Q4. It is necessary for a function which receives variable number of arguments, must receive at least one fixed argument. [True/False]

ANSWER: True.

Q5. The fixed argument passed to a function that receives variable number of arguments can be at the end of the argument list. [True/False]

ANSWER: False. We can never have the fixed argument at the end of the argument list.

Q6. What will be the output of below C code?

```c
#include <stdio.h>

#include <stdarg.h>

void func (int,...);

int main()

{

func (5, 1, 2, 3, 0, 7);

return 0;

}

void func (int num,...)

{

int sum = 0, j;

va_list ptr;

va_start (ptr, num);

for (j = 1; j <= num; ++j)

sum += va_arg (ptr, int);

printf ("Total sum is: %d", sum);

}
```

ANSWER: Total sum is: 13

See how func () has been declared. The ellipses (...) indicate that the number of arguments after the first fixed argument will be variable. The value of fixed argument is 5 and has been stored in variable **num** and function definition begins with a declaration of a pointer **ptr** of type **va_list**. The macro **va_start ()** initializes the **ptr** to point to the first variable of argument in the list. Hence, **ptr** would point to 1 in our case. Also, the statement **sum +=** **va_arg (ptr, int)** will assign the integer value being pointed to by **ptr** to **sum** in fact value returned by **va_arg ()** are being added to **sum** and **ptr** would point to next integer variable.

Q7. What will be the output of below C code?

```
#include <stdio.h>

#include <stdarg.h>

void func1 (int,...);

void func2 (int,...);

int main()

{

func1 (3, "Java", "Perl", "Ruby");

func2 (3, 4500, 2500, 3000);

return 0;

}

void func1 (int num,...)

{

va_list ptr;

char *str;

va_start (ptr, num);

str = va_arg (ptr, char *);
```

```c
printf ("%s ", str);

}
void func2 (int num,...)

{
va_list ptr;

int val;

va_start (ptr, num);

val = va_arg (ptr, int);

printf ("%d", val);

}
```

ANSWER: Java 4500

Q8. What will be the output of below C code?

```c
#include <stdio.h>

#include <stdarg.h>

void func (int,...);

int main()

{
func (4, 5, 6, 7, 8);

return 0;

}
void func (int num,...)

{
```

```c
va_list ptr;

int val;

val = va_arg (ptr, int);

printf ("%d", val);

}
```

ANSWER: The program would cause an Exception at run time.

The statement- **va_start (ptr, num);** is missing in our program hence pointer **ptr** may be pointing to somewhere else and this will cause a run time exception.

Q9. What will be the output of below C code?

```c
#include <stdio.h>

#include <stdarg.h>

void func (int num,...);

int main()

{

func (4, "Say", "hello", "to", "C");

return 0;

}

void func (int num,...)

{

char *ptr;

va_start (ptr, num);

char *str = va_arg (ptr, char *);
```

printf ("%s", str);

}

ANSWER: Say

Did you notice? We have used **char** *ptr instead of **va_list** to declare a pointer **ptr** in our question. Many modern compilers like Ideone and codepad will not give any error. Program works fine.

Q10. Can we have a following function declaration in C which takes variable number of arguments?

void func (…)

{

/* some codes */

}

ANSWER: No.

According to C standard, at least one fixed argument must be supplied to the function so that you can hand it to **va_start**. (In any case, you often need a fixed argument to determine the number, and perhaps the types, of the variable arguments.)

Q11. What will be the output of below C code?

#include <stdio.h>

#include <stdarg.h>

void func (int num,…);

int main()

{

func (4, 'a', 'b', 'c', 'd');

```c
return 0;
}
void func (int num,...)
{
char ch1, ch2;
int i;
va_list ptr1;
va_list ptr2;
va_start (ptr1, num);
va_start (ptr2, num);
for (i = 1; i <= num; ++i)
{
ch1 = va_arg (ptr1, int);  /* why int is being passed instead of char */
printf ("%c ", ch1);
ch2 = va_arg (ptr2, int);
printf ("%d\n", ch2);
}
}
```

ANSWER: a 97

               b 98

               c 99

               d 100

Q12. What will be the output of below C code?

```c
#include <stdio.h>
#include <stdarg.h>
void func (int num,...);
int main()
{
func (4, 'A', 'B', 'C', 'D');
return 0;
}
void func (int num,...)
{
char ch;
int j;
va_list ptr;
va_start (ptr, num);
for (j = 1; j <= num; ++j)
{
ch = va_arg (ptr, char);
printf ("%c ", ch);
}
}
```

ANSWER: Compile time error.

Many beginners say that as we are passing variable number of arguments of **char** type so the statement- **va_arg (ptr, char);** is perfectly fine but according to C standard in a variable-length argument list, the "default argument promotions" rule gets applied : types **char** and **short int** are promoted to **int**, and **float** is promoted to **double**. Therefore, **printf** ()'s %f format always sees a **double** and in the same way, %c always sees an **int**. Okay, but still compilation error, compiler should have promoted that **char** to **int**. But it did not, why? Well, to know the reason, read the below lines-

When a function accepts a variable number of arguments, its prototype does not (and cannot) provide any information about the number and types of those variable arguments. Therefore, the usual protections don't apply in the variable-length part of variable-length argument lists: the compiler cannot perform implicit conversions or (in general) warn about mismatches. The programmer must make sure that arguments match, or must manually insert explicit casts. That is why we are getting compile time error. To successfully compile the program, replace **char** by **int**. Also, did you notice the comment mentioned in Q11? I think it's clear now. These concepts are rarely found in any textbooks available in the market these days.

Q13. Is there any way to discover, how many arguments a function was actually called with?

ANSWER: No.

Any function, which takes variable number of arguments can determine the number of arguments supplied to it, from those arguments only. The standard library function **printf** () does this by looking for format specifier **(%s, %d, %c etc.)**. That is why such functions fail in case of any mismatch between format specifier and the argument list.

Q14. What will be the output of below C code?

#include <stdio.h>

#include <stdarg.h>

```c
void func (int num,...);

int main()

{
func (3, 3.14, 1.414, 0.333);

return 0;

}
void func (int num,...)

{
float ft = 0.0;

int i;

va_list ptr;

va_start (ptr, num);

for (i = 1; i <= num; ++i)

ft += va_arg (ptr, float);

printf ("%f", ft);

}
```

ANSWER: Compilation error.

In function 'void func(int, ...)': [Warning] 'float' is promoted to 'double' when passed through '...' [Warning] (so you should pass 'double' not 'float' to 'va_arg') if this code is reached, the program will abort. This what compiler gives on compiling this code. To successfully compile this program, try replacing **float** by **double**.

Q15. What will be the output of below C code?

#include <stdio.h>

```c
#include <stdarg.h>

void func (char *, char *, int, char *,...);

int main()

{

func ("Say", "hello", 2, "Java", 3.14, 1.414, 0.333);

return 0;

}

void func (char *str1, char *str2, int num, char *str3,...)

{

double val;

va_list ptr;

va_start (ptr, str1);

val = va_arg (ptr, double);

printf ("%lf", val);

}
```

ANSWER: 3.140000 with a warning- In function 'void func(char*, char*, int, char*, ...)' [Warning] second parameter of 'va_start' not last named argument. Compliers like Ideone and codepad won't even give any warning. It is better to set the **ptr** to the last fixed argument. So, **va_start (ptr, str3)** should be used in our program to ignore the warning.

Q16. Can we have a function which takes a variable argument list and passes the list to another function also takes a variable number of arguments?

ANSWER: Yes, we can have but the syntax is quite different for doing this. See Q17 which implements this concept.

Q17. What will be the output of below C code?

```c
#include <stdio.h>
#include <stdarg.h>
void func1 (int,...);
void func2 (int, va_list ptr1);
int main()
{
func1 (4, 11, 22, 33, 44);
return 0;
}
void func1 (int num,...)
{
va_list ptr;
va_start (ptr, num);
func2 (num, ptr);
}
void func2 (int num, va_list ptr1)
{
int x, y, z;
x = num;
for (z = 1; z <= x; ++z)
{
```

```
y = va_arg (ptr1, int);

printf ("%d ", y);

}

}
```

ANSWER: 11 22 33 44

Clearly, the arguments which were supplied to **func1** (), gets printed in **func2** (). See, the prototype declaration of **func2** ().

Chapter-13

Complicated Declarations In C

Q1. What is a complex declarator in C?

ANSWER: In C, a complex declarator is an identifier qualified by more than one array, pointer, or function modifier. You can apply various combinations of array, pointer, and function modifiers to a single identifier.

Rules for interpreting complex declarators-

In interpreting complex declarators, brackets and parentheses (that is, modifiers to the right of the identifier) take precedence over asterisks (that is, modifiers to the left of the identifier). Brackets and parentheses have the same precedence and associate from left to right. After the declarator has been fully interpreted, the type specifier is applied as the last step. By using parentheses you can override the default association order and force a particular interpretation. Never use parentheses, however, around an identifier name by itself. This could be misinterpreted as a parameter list.

A simple way to interpret complex declarators is to read them "from the inside out", using the following four steps:

1. Start with the identifier and look directly to the right for brackets or parentheses (if any).

2. Interpret these brackets or parentheses, and then look to the left for asterisks.

3. If you encounter a right parenthesis at any stage, go back and apply rules 1 and 2 to everything within the parentheses.

4. Apply the type specifier.

We will apply these rules for solving many questions on complex declarators.

Q2. What does the following declaration signify in C?

char * (* (*var) ( )) [10];
    7 6 4 2 1 3   5

ANSWER: After numbering in order, the declaration can be interpreted as-

var * ( ) * [10] * char

Read from left to right as-

"var is a pointer to a function returning a pointer to an array of 10 elements which are pointers to **char**."

Q3. What does the following declaration signify in C?

int (*fptr) ( );

ANSWER: Firstly number the identifiers in order as shown below-

int (*fptr) ( );
4 2 1 3

fptr * ( ) int

Read from left to right as-

"fptr is a pointer to a function returning **int**."

Q4. What does the following declaration signify in C?

int (*ptr)[10];

ANSWER: Firstly number the identifiers in order as shown below-

int (* ptr) [10];
4 2 1 3

ptr * [10] int

Read from left to right as-

"ptr is pointer to an array of 10 integers."

Q5. What does the following declaration signify in C?

void (*arr[5]) (int, int);

ANSWER: void (*arr[5]) (int, int);

```
        5    3 1 2      4
```

arr [5] * (int, int) void

Read from left to right as-

"arr is an array of 5 function pointers, each pointer points to a function that receives two integers as parameters and returns nothing."

Q6. What does the following declaration signify in C?

float * (*ptr) (int *);

ANSWER: float * (* ptr) (int *);

```
        4      2  1      3
```

ptr * (int *) float *

"ptr is a pointer to a function which takes an integer pointer and returns a pointer to a float".

Q7. What does the following declaration signify in C?

char (* (* x()) []) ();

ANSWER: char (* (* x ()) []) ();

```
        7     5  3 1 2    4  6
```

x () * [] * () char

" x is a function returning pointer to an array of pointers to function returning char."

Q8. What does the following declaration signify in C?

    int (*(*func_one)(char *, double))[9][20];

ANSWER: int (* (* func_one) (char*, double)) [9][20];

           6   4 2 1   3   5

func_one * (char *, double) * [9][20] int

"func_one is a pointer to a function which receives a char pointer and a double as parameters and returns a pointer to an array (size 9) of array (size 20) of int".

Q9. What does the following declaration signify in C?

    char (* (*x[3]) ())[5];

ANSWER: char (* (* x[3]) ()) [5];

        7   5 3 1 2 4 6

x [3] * () * [5] char

"x is an array of 3 pointers to function returning pointer to an array of 5 char".

Q10. What does the following declaration signify in C?

    int *(* (*arr[5]) ()) ();

ANSWER: int *(* (*arr[5]) ()) ();

        8 7 5 3 1 2   4 6

arr [5] * () * () * int

"arr is an array of 5 function pointers returning pointer to a function returning pointer to an integer."

Q11. What does the following declaration signify in C?

   void (*func)(int, void(*)());

ANSWER: void (*func)(int, void(*) ());
            ↑   ↑ ↑   ↑
            4   2 1   3

func * (int, void(*) ()) void

func is pointer to a function which returns nothing and receives as its parameter an integer and a pointer to a function which receives nothing and returns nothing.

Q12. Is the following declaration legal in C?

   int *((*func_one) ()) [][];

ANSWER: int *((* func_one) ()) [][];
           ↑ ↑ ↑   ↑   ↑ ↑
           6 5 2   1   3 4

func_one * () [][] * int

"func_one is a pointer to function returning an array of array of pointer to integers."

This is what the function declaration means. Since a function cannot return an array, but only a pointer to an array, this declaration is illegal.

Note: - Illegal combinations include:

   1. []() - cannot have an array of functions.

   2. ()() - cannot have a function that returns a function.

   3. ()[] - cannot have a function that returns an array.

Q13. Is the following declaration legal in C?

   int *afp [] ();

ANSWER: No, it's an invalid declaration.

It is an array of functions returning int pointers and we know that an array of functions is not possible. Hence it's not a valid declaration.

Q14. Is the following declaration legal in C?

int afa [] () [];

ANSWER: No, it's not a valid declaration.

It is an array of functions returning an array of ints. Since a function can't return an array hence it is not a valid declaration.

Q15. What does the following declaration signify in C?

char * (* (**foo [][8]) ())[];

ANSWER: char * (* (* * foo [][8]) ())[];

9 8 6 4 3 1 2 5 7

foo [][8] * * () * [] * char

"foo is array of array of 8 pointer to pointer to a function returning pointer to array of pointer to char".

Chapter-14

Memory Management In C

Q1. What are the differences between malloc () and calloc ()?

ANSWER: Both **malloc** () and **calloc** () are standard library function defined in **stdlib.h** header file and are used for memory allocation from **heap** an area of memory (RAM) structured for this purpose during run time. The two main differences between **malloc** () and **calloc** () are-

First, **malloc** () takes a single argument (the amount of memory to allocate in bytes), while **calloc** () needs two arguments (the number of variables to allocate in memory, and the size in bytes of a single variable). Secondly, **malloc** () does not initialize the memory allocated, while **calloc** () initializes all bytes of the allocated memory block to zero.

For example-

int *ptr = (int *)malloc (10 * sizeof(int)); will allocate memory for 10 integers whereas

int *ptr = (int *)calloc (10, sizeof(int)); will also allocate memory for 10 integers.

Q2. What is realloc () in C?

ANSWER: **realloc** () is a standard library function defined in **stdlib.h** header and is used for changing the size of dynamically allocated memory.

void *realloc (void *ptr, size_t size);

The function **realloc** () reallocates a memory block with a specific new size. If you call **realloc** () the size of the memory block pointed to by the pointer is changed to the given size in bytes. Also it is possible that the function moves the memory block to a new location, in which way the function will return this new location. If the size of the requested block is larger than the previous block then the value of the new portion is indeterminate.

Note: - **realloc** () should only be used for dynamically allocated memory. If the memory is not dynamically allocated, then behaviour is undefined.

Q3. What is free () in C? How does free () know the size of memory to be deallocated?

ANSWER: **free** () is a standard library function defined in **stdlib.h** header file and is used to deallocate the block of memory previously allocated by a call to **malloc** (), **calloc** () or **realloc** ().

void free (void *ptr);

1. If **ptr** does not point to a block of memory allocated with the above functions, it causes undefined behaviour.

2. If **ptr** is a null pointer, then the function does nothing.

Clearly **free** () function does not accept size as a parameter but still it deallocates the allocated memory easily. The answer is- "When memory allocation is done, the actual **heap** space allocated is one word larger than the requested memory. The extra word is used to store the size of the allocation and is later used by **free** ( )" and this extra word is stored adjacent to the allocated bloc of memory.

Q4. When does the function realloc () behave like malloc () and free ()?

ANSWER: 1. If the pointer is **NULL** then the function will behave exactly like the function **malloc** (). It will assign a new block of a size in bytes and will return a pointer to it.

2. If the size is **0** then the memory that was previously allocated is freed as if a call of the function **free** () was given. It will return a **NULL** pointer in that case.

Q5. What is memory leak in C?

ANSWER: A memory leak in computer science (or leakage in this context), occurs when a computer program consumes memory but is unable to release it back to the operating system. Memory leaks are a common error in programming, especially when using languages that have no built in automatic garbage collection, such as C and C++. Typically, a memory leak occurs because dynamically allocated memory has become unreachable.

Q6. What is wrong with following C code?

#include <stdio.h>

int main()

{

int *ptr = (int *)malloc(sizeof (int));

ptr = NULL;

free(ptr);

return 0;

}

ANSWER: The code will suffer from memory leak. Since, **malloc** () has allocated memory and its reference has been assigned to pointer **ptr** but soon **ptr** becomes a null pointer but allocated memory in not freed which results into memory leakage. The correct way should be like-

1. **free(ptr);** then

2. **ptr = NULL;**

Q7. Is it always necessary to typecast the return type of malloc () in C?

ANSWER: It is necessary if you are using TC/TC++ or an MS Visual Studio compiler but there is **no** need of typecasting in case of **gcc** compilers.

Q8. What is wrong with following C code?

```c
#include <stdio.h>
#include <stdlib.h>
int main()
{
union test
{
int i;
float f;
char *s;
};
union test *t;
t = (union test *)malloc(sizeof(union test));
t->s = (char *)malloc(20);
t->s = "Hello";
free(t);
printf ("%s", t->s);
return 0;
}
```

ANSWER: Garbage Value will be printed on console.

After executing **free(t)**, pointer **t** becomes a dangling pointer and we are accessing the union member using this pointer which is no longer available and hence program gives unpredictable result.

Q9. What will be the output of below C code?

```c
#include <stdio.h>
#include <string.h>
char * func()
{
char arr[30];
strcpy (arr, "It will not work"));
return arr;
}
int main()
{
char *str = func();
printf ("%s", str);
return 0;
}
```

ANSWER: Nothing will be printed on console.

Some compilers may give a warning- 'address of local variable '**arr**' returned.

Array **arr** is having **auto** storage class and hence the control comes to **main** (), the array **arr** will be no more available and thus **str** will be pointing to an array which is no longer exist.

Q10. Can we increase the size of a statically allocated array in C?

ANSWER: No.

Q11. In the following C code, where the variables i, j and k are stored in memory?

#include <stdio.h>

int i;

int main()

{

int j;

int *k = (int *)malloc(sizeof(int));

return 0;

}

ANSWER: Variable **i** will be stored in **BSS** Segment of Data Segment of RAM, variable **j** will be stored in **Stack** Segment whereas variable **k** will be stored in **Heap** Segment of RAM.

Q12. What are the different types of Program Memory in C?

ANSWER: The computer program memory is organized into the following:

1. Data Segment (Data + BSS + Heap)

2. Stack

3. Code segment

Data- The data area contains global and static variables used by the program that are explicitly initialized with a value. This segment can be further classified into a read-only area and read-write area. For instance, the string defined by char s[] = "hello world" in C and a C statement like **int** debug = 1 outside the "main" would be stored in initialized read-write area. And a C statement like **const** char *string = "hello world" makes the string literal "hello world" to be stored in initialized read-only area and the character pointer variable string in initialized read-write area. Ex: both static int i = 10 and global int i = 10 will be stored in the data segment.

BSS- Also known as uninitialized data, starts at the end of the data segment and contains all global variables and static variables that are initialized to zero or do not have explicit initialization in source code. For instance a variable declared **static int** i; would be contained in the **BSS** segment.

Heap- The heap area begins at the end of the **BSS segment** and grows to larger addresses from there. The heap area is managed by malloc, realloc, and free. The heap area is shared by all shared libraries and dynamically loaded modules in a process.

Stack- The stack area contains the program stack, a LIFO structure, typically located in the higher parts of memory. A "stack pointer" register tracks the top of the stack; it is adjusted each time a value is "pushed" onto the stack. The set of values pushed for one function call is termed a "stack frame". A stack frame consists at minimum of a return address. Automatic variables are also allocated on the stack.

Q13. What do you mean by segmentation fault in C? Also mention the causes of segmentation fault in C?

ANSWER: A segmentation fault occurs when a program attempts to access a memory location that it is not allowed to access, or attempts to access a memory location in a way that is not allowed (for example, attempting to write to a read-only location, or to overwrite part of the operating system).

The following are some typical causes of a segmentation fault:

1. Attempting to execute a program that does not compile correctly. Some compilers will output an executable file despite the presence of compile-time errors.

2. Dereferencing **NULL** pointers

3. Attempting to access memory the program does not have rights to (such as kernel structures in process context)

4. Attempting to access a nonexistent memory address (outside process's address space)

5. Attempting to write read-only memory (such as code segment)

6. A buffer overflow

7. Using uninitialized pointers

Q14. What will be the output of below C code?

```
#include <stdio.h>
#include <stdlib.h>
#define ROW 3
#define COL 3
int main()
{
int (*ptr)[COL];
ptr = (int (*)[COL])malloc(sizeof(ROW * sizeof(*ptr));
printf ("%d %d", sizeof(ptr), sizeof(*ptr));
return 0;
}
```

ANSWER: 4 12 (On 32-bit system)

Q15. Replace Line 1 and Line 2 with suitable C statements so that program doesn't cause any memory leak.

```
#include <stdio.h>
```

```
#include <stdlib.h>

int main()

{

struct demo

{

int x;

float f;

char *str;

};

struct demo *ptr;

ptr = (struct demo *)malloc(sizeof(struct demo));

ptr -> str = (char *)malloc(sizeof(20));

/* Line 1 */

/* Line 2 */

return 0;

}
```

ANSWER: free(ptr -> str); → Line 1

        free(ptr); → Line 2

70032	70036	70040
For variable **i**	For variable **f**	65512

ptr -> i   ptr -> f   ptr -> str

70032

8004   Dynamically Allocated

Hello

65512

Chapter-15

Miscellaneous Concepts

Q1. What will be the output of below C code?

#include <stdio.h>

int main()

{

int x = 14;

x = x & (x - 1);

printf ("%d", x);

return 0;

}

ANSWER: 12

The given expression **x & (x - 1)** turns off the rightmost set bit. Binary equivalent of decimal 14 is- (1110) which gets changed to decimal 12 whose binary equivalent is- (1100).

Q2. What will be the output of below C code?

#include <stdio.h>

int main()

{

int x = 8, count = 0;

while (x)

{

```
x = x & (x - 1);

++count;

}

printf ("%d", count);

return 0;

}
```

ANSWER: 1

This program counts the number of set bits in the given decimal value i, e 8. Binary equivalent of **8** is- (**1000**) and binary equivalent of **7** (**8-1**) is (**0111**). Initially **while** () loop is true because **x** is **8**. Now the value of expression (**1000**) & (**0111**) will be (**0000**) i, e decimal **0** which is being assigned to **x**. Hence next time loop gets false and **printf** () prints the final value of **count** which is **1**.

Q3. What will be the output of below C code?

```
#include <stdio.h>

int main()

{

int x = 4;

if (x & 1)

printf ("Odd");

else

printf ("Even");

return 0;

}
```

ANSWER: Even

This is an efficient way checking whether a given number is even or odd. Binary equivalent of 4 is- (0100). The expression **(x & 1)** is **(0100 & 0001)** which yields **(0000)** in case **x** is even whereas **(0001)** in case **x** is odd.

Q4. What will be the output of below C code?

```c
#include <stdio.h>

int main()

{

int x = 16;

if (x && ( !(x & (x - 1)))

printf ("Yes");

else

printf ("No");

return 0;

}
```

ANSWER: Yes

This program checks whether the given number is a power of 2 or not. Decimals like 16 (4^2), 64 (8^2) etc are power of 2. If the expression **(x & (x - 1))** is zero then the given number will be a power of 2. If a number is exact power of 2, it will have only one 1-bit in its binary equivalent. Bit pattern of 16 (00000000 00000000 00000000 00010000) and bit pattern of 256 (00000000 00000000 00000001 00000000) have only one 1-bit.

Q5. The effect of shifting one bit right of an unsigned **int** or **char** is equivalent to integer division by 2. [True/False]

ANSWER: True

Q6. The effect of shifting one bit left of an unsigned **int** or **char** is equivalent to integer multiplication by 2. [True/False]

ANSWER: True

Q7. Write your own version of **sizeof** () operator in C.

ANSWER:

#include <stdio.h>

#define SIZEOF(var) (size_t) ((char *)(&var + 1) - (char *)(&var))

int main()

{

int i;

printf ("%d", SIZEOF(i));

return 0;

}

ANSWER: 4 (On 32-bit system)

As we know that **sizeof** () yields the size of its operand with respect to the size of type **char**. Suppose variable **i** is located at **2686788** memory location hence (**&i + 1**) will be **2686792** as **int** is 4 bytes long on a 32-bit system.

Q8. What will be the output of below C code?

#include <stdio.h>

int func ()

{

return (printf ("Hello World"));

}

```
int main()

{

printf ("%d", sizeof (func));

return 0;

}
```

ANSWER: 4

As we know **sizeof** () is a compile time operator but not a function. Hence **func** () won't be called. But compiler is giving 4 why? It is because in C, function name is treated as a pointer which holds the address of function. In C, functions also have the address just like **int, char**, and **float** etc. **sizeof** () of a pointer would give 4.

Q9. What will be the output of below C code?

```
#include <stdio.h>

int main()

{

printf ("%d %d", 3 >> 1, 8 >> 1);

return 0;

}
```

ANSWER: 1 4

Q10. What will be the output of below C code?

```
#include <stdio.h>

int main()

{

typedef int x
```

x i = 12;

printf ("%d", i);

return 0;

}

ANSWER: 12

typedef is a keyword in C which is use to redefine the name of an existing variable type. In this program, data type **int** has been given a new name **x** for further uses and program works fine.

Q11. What is the type of var1 and var2 in following code segment?

typedef unsigned long int LONG_INT

LONG_INT var1, var2

ANSWER: var1 and var2 are of **unsigned long int** type. Usually uppercase letters are used to make it clear that we are dealing with a redefined data type i, e typedef.

Q12. What is the type of func_ptr in the following declaration?

typedef void (*ptrtofunc)(int *, int *);

ptrtofunc func_ptr;

ANSWER: **func_ptr** is a pointer to a function that receives two integer pointers and returns nothing.

Q13. What is the type of ptr in the following code segment?

typedef int * p;

const p ptr;

ANSWER: **ptr** is a constant pointer to a non-const integer.

Q14. What is the type of ptr2 in the following code segment?

```c
typedef char * ptr;

ptr ptr1, ptr2;
```

ANSWER: **ptr2** is a character pointer.

Q15. What will be the output of below C code?

```c
#include <stdio.h>

int main()

{

typedef enum languages {java, perl, lisp, ruby} LANG;

LANG lang = perl;

printf ("%d", lang);

return 0;

}
```

ANSWER: 1

Q16. What is the type of ptr1, ptr2, ptr3 and ptr4 in the following code segment?

```c
typedef float * float_t;

#define float_d float *

float_t  ptr1, ptr2;

float_d  ptr3, ptr4;
```

ANSWER: **ptr1**, **ptr2** and **ptr3** are of float pointer whereas **ptr4** is of float type.

Q17. What is the type of **var** in the following code segment?

```c
typedef char * ( * (*ptr) ( ) ) [10];
```

ptr var;

ANSWER: **"var** is a pointer to a function returning a pointer to an array of 10 elements which are pointers to **char**."

Q18. What will be the output of below C code?

```
#include <stdio.h>

int main()

{

typedef int * i;

int j = 20;

i *k = &j;

printf("%d", **k);

return 0

}
```

ANSWER: Compile time error- "cannot convert 'int*' to 'int**' in initialization".

Due to the line *typedef* **int * i**, variable **k** becomes a pointer to a pointer i,e **k** will hold the address of a pointer variable but instead it holds the address of a simple integer variable **j**. The type mismatch leads to compilation error.

Q19. What will be the output of below C code?

```
#include <stdio.h>

int main()

{

typedef static int *i;

int j;
```

i k = &j;

printf("%d", *k);

return 0;

}

ANSWER: Compile time error.

In C, *typedef* is considered as a storage class just like auto, static, extern etc. We are not allowed to have multiple storage class for a variable.

Q20. What is the error in the following structure declaration?

typedef struct

{

int num;

PTR next;

} *PTR;

ANSWER: The statement PTR next is an erroneous line because a typedef declaration can't be used until it is defined. When the **next** field was declared then at that point of time *typedef* declaration was not done.

Note:- There are three ways of removing this error-

1. typedef struct Node

{

int num;

struct Node *next;

} *PTR;

2. struct Node

```
{

int num;

struct Node *next;

};

typedef struct Node *PTR;

3. typedef struct node *PTR;

struct Node

{

int num;

PTR next;

};
```

Q21. **#defines** always have a global effect whereas *typedefs* can be made local to a function or a block i, e their scopes can be localized. [True/False]

ANSWER: True.

Q22. What will be the output of below C code?

```
#include <stdio.h>

typedef int * p;

typedef int i;

int main()

{

p func (i, i);

i a = 2;

i b = 2;
```

printf ("%d", *func (a, b));

return 0;

}

p func (i x, i y)

{

static i val = x + y;

return (&val);

}

ANSWER: 4

Q23. What will be the output of below C code?

#include <stdio.h>

int main()

{

int x = -12;

x = x >> 3;

printf ("%d", x);

return 0;

}

ANSWER: -2

Here variable **x** is negative hence -12 will be stored in 2's complement form in the memory. Binary equivalent of -12 is- 11111111 11110100 (consider **int** takes 2 bytes) then right shift all bits by 3 places and then fill first three empty space by 1. The bit pattern will look like as-

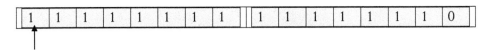

It is again a negative number hence its 2's complement will be- 00000000 00000010 and hence final output will be -2

Q24. What will be the output of below C code?

```c
#include <stdio.h>

int main()

{

const int x;

x = 100;

printf ("%d", x);

return 0;

}
```

ANSWER: Compile time error.

A **const** variable can be given a value only through initialization. Hence, **x** must have been be initialized when it is defined. Actually, variables having **const** qualifier gets stored in a special section of RAM which is known as "Data Segment" and this segment is further classified into a read-only area and write-only area. In our case variable **x** would be stored in initialized read-only area. Once stored, we can only read but can never write or alter. Variables of **non-const** types are also stored in "Data Segment" but in read-write area. We can easily alter their values.

Q25. What will be the output of below C code?

```c
#include <stdio.h>

int main()
```

```
{
int x = 10;
int * const ptr = &x;
++(*ptr);
printf("%d", x);
return 0;
}
```

ANSWER: 11

Here **ptr** is **const** but the integer to which it is pointing, is not **const**. Hence we can alter the value of **x** but we can never alter the pointer **ptr**. Also **ptr** is not Lvalue here and hence we can't do any arithmetic operation on **ptr**.

Q26. What will be the output of below C code?

```
#include <stdio.h>
int main()
{
int x = 10;
int const * ptr = &x;
++(*ptr);
printf("%d", x);
return 0;
}
```

ANSWER: Compile time error.

Here, pointer **ptr** is not **const** but to which it is pointing, is **const**. We can alter the pointer **ptr** but we can't alter the value of variable **x**. In this program we are trying to change the value of **x** by incrementing it which is not allowed.

Q27. What will be the output of below C code?

```
#include <stdio.h>

int main()

{
char str[] = "Hello";

const char * const ptr = "Java";

ptr = str;

*ptr = 'W';

return 0;

}
```

ANSWER: Compile time error.

We can neither alter the pointer **ptr** nor the object it is pointing to. Both are of **const** type.

Q28. The following declarations are same. [True/False]

```
const int * const ptr;

int const * const ptr;
```

ANSWER: True.

Q29. What will be the output of below C code?

```
#include <stdio.h>
```

```
int main()

{

int arr[] = {1, 2, 3, 4, 5, 6};

int *ptr1 = &arr[0];

int *ptr2 = arr + 5;

printf ("%d", (char *)ptr2 - (char *)ptr1);

return 0;

}
```

ANSWER: 20 (On 32-bit system in bytes)

ptr1 and **ptr2** are pointing to 0th and 5th element of the given array hence both pointers are 5 integers apart. But **ptr1** and **ptr2** are of **(char *)** type hence we will consider every 1 byte of each element of the array. Since we have 5 integers between **ptr1** and **ptr2** and each element comprises of 4 bytes (32-bit system) so considering **(char *)** there is a total of (5 * 4) bytes i, e 20 bytes. In simple words, **sizeof (int) * 5** is our answer because both pointers are 5 integers apart.

Q30. What will be the output of below C code?

```
#include <stdio.h>

int main()

{

const int x = 12;

int * const ptr = &x;

printf ("%d", *ptr);

return 0;
```

}

ANSWER: Compile time error- 'Invalid conversion from 'const int*' to 'int*'.

Initially variable **x** has been made constant but while declaring pointer **ptr**, we missed to use **const** before expression- int * const ptr = &x; And hence compiler thinks that we are trying to convert **x** from **const int** to **int** which leads to compilation error. The correct way is- **const int * const ptr = &x;**

Q31. What will be the output of below C code?

```
#include <stdio.h>

void func (int *, const int *, int *);

int main()

{

int arr1[] = {1, 2, 3, 4};

int arr2[] = {5, 8, 3, 2};

int arr3[] = {7, 6, 5, 4};

func (arr1, arr2, arr3);

printf ("%d", arr3[0]);

return 0;

}

void func (int *arr1, const int *arr2, int *arr3)

{

arr1 = arr3;

++arr1[0];
```

arr2 = arr3;

++arr2[0];

}

ANSWER: Compile time error.

Inside **func** (), **arr1**, **arr2** and **arr3** are pointers. Also **arr2** is of **const** type hence the statement **++arr2[0]** is erroneous because through this statement we are trying to modify the 0th element of array **arr3[]** which is now **const** because the reference in **arr3** has been assigned to **arr2**.

Q32. What will be the output of below C code?

```
#include <stdio.h>

int func *()

{

int *ptr = (int *)malloc (sizeof(int));

return ptr;

}

int main ()

{

const int *q = func();

*q = 11;

printf ("%d", *q);

return 0;

}
```

ANSWER: Compile time error.

malloc () not only allocates memory but also initializes all memory location with a garbage value. Inside **main** (), the statement **const int *q = func()** makes those values as **const** which can't be altered later.

Q33. What will be the output of below C code?

#include <stdio.h>

int main()

{

double x;

(float)(int)(char) x;

printf ("%d", sizeof ((int)(float)(char) x));

return 0;

}

ANSWER: 4

Initially variable **x** was declared of type **double** and then typecasted into **char**, **int** and **float** respectively. No problem, we can typecast as many times, we want. Inside **printf** (), **x** is being typecasted again but this time final data type of variable **x** is **int** which takes 4 bytes of memory.

Q34. What will be the output of below C code?

#include <stdio.h>

int main()

{

int (*q)[2][4];

printf ("%d", sizeof(*q));

return 0;

}

ANSWER: 32

Here, **q** is a pointer to a 2-D array of 2 rows and 4 columns. But **(*q)** means an array of 2 rows and 4 columns which takes **2 * 4 * sizeof (int)** i, e 32 bytes of memory.

Q35. Write the correct prototype declaration of malloc ()?

ANSWER: void * malloc (size_t size);

Q36. What will be the output of below C code?

#include <stdio.h>

void func();

int main()

{

void (*func_ptr)();

func_ptr = func;

printf ("Address of func is: %u", func_ptr);

func_ptr();

return 0;

}

void func()

{

printf ("Hello C");

}

ANSWER: Hello C

In this program we have declared a function pointer **func_ptr**. The declaration says- **func_ptr** is a pointer to a function which accepts nothing and also returns nothing. Do remember the parentheses around **func_ptr**, in absence of these, **func_ptr** will become a function which takes nothing but returns a **void** pointer. We have assigned the address of function **func** () to **func_ptr** to invoke **func** (). See how **func** () has been called, we have to only write the statement **func_ptr()**. We can also write (***func_ptr**) to invoke **func** ().

Q37. What will be the output of below C code?

#include <stdio.h>

#include <stdlib.h>

#include <string.h>

char *func1(char* (*fp)());

char *func2();

int main()

{

char *(*fptr)();

fptr = func2;

printf ("%s", func1(fptr));

return 0;

}

char *func1(char *(*fp)())

{

return ((*fp)());

}

```c
char *func2()

{

char *str = (char *)malloc(20);

strcpy(str, "Hello World");

return (str);

}
```

ANSWER: Hello World

Try to figure out this question at your own. This question also deals with pointer to a function. We have two functions here whose prototypes have clearly mentioned. If you do this at your own, then you can tackle any question based on function's pointer in future.

Q38. What will be the output of below C code?

```c
#include <stdio.h>

unsigned long int (* func() )[3]

{

static unsigned long int arr[3] = {11, 22, 33};

return (&arr);

}

int main()

{

unsigned long int (*q)[3];

q = func();

printf ("%d", (*q)[2]);
```

return 0;

}

ANSWER: 33

Here **func** () is a function which returns a pointer to an array of 3 elements of **unsigned long int** type. Also, **q** is a pointer to an array of 3 elements of **unsigned long int** type. **func** () returns the address of array **arr** which is being assigned to pointer **q**. Using **q**, we are accessing the 3rd element of array **arr**. Expression **(*q)[2]** is not a mystery now because we have done a lot of problems like this in Chapter 7.

Q39. What will be the output of below C code?

```
#include <stdio.h>

char _x_ (int, ...);

int main()

{

char (*ptr)(int, ...) = &_x_;

for (; (*ptr)(0, 1, 2, 3, 4) ;)

printf ("%d", +2);

return 0;

}

char _x_(int x, ...)

{

static int i = -1;

return (i + ++ x);

}
```

ANSWER: Nothing will be printed on console.

Here _x_ is a variadic function, you know why? Also **ptr** is a pointer to the function _x_() and inside **for** loop the test condition **(*ptr)(0, 1, 2, 3, 4)** is nothing but _x_(0, 1, 2, 3, 4) because ***** and **&** always cancel each other. Function _x_ is called first time by passing 0 as argument. _x_ returns (-1 + ++x) which is equivalent to (-1 + 1) i, e **0** which is **false** in C hence **for** loop gets false and **printf** () is not executed.

Q40. What will be the output of below C code?

```c
#include <stdio.h>
#include <stdarg.h>
void show (char *str, ...);
int func1();
int func2();
int main()
{
int (*ptr1)();
int (*ptr2)();
ptr1 = func1();
ptr2 = func2();
show ("Hello", ptr1, ptr2);
return 0;
}
void show (char *s, ...)
{
```